W9-DGK-683

Being Saved

Being Saved

Peter Mullen

SCM PRESS LTD

British Library Cataloguing-in-Publication Data available

334 01894 3

First published 1985
by SCM Press Ltd
26–30 Tottenham Road, London N1

Phototypeset by Input Typesetting Ltd

Printed and bound in Great Britain
by Billing & Sons Limited, Worcester.

Contents

Introduction

How strange that, in our secular society, religion is never out of the news! And yet not so strange because, for good or ill, the Christian religion in its words, pictures and music has shaped life in this country for more than a thousand years. It is comparatively recently that the superstition has arisen about 'religion disproved by science'. But it is this half-articulated suspicion which has divided Christian believing into what looks like two distinct and opposing camps. The liberals and radicals seem to spend much of their time saying, 'But that I can't believe!' revising, demythologizing and modernizing the faith to such a degree that it has become distilled into a bloodless intellectual essence, hardly worth believing in at all. Partly in reaction to the liberals, there has been a resurgence of literalism and fundamentalism which often seems to dodge criticism and honest questioning to the point where its adherents are like the Red Queen in *Alice* who could 'believe six impossible things before breakfast'.

Like most parsons of my generation I grew up and received my theological training in this atmosphere of tension. But for a long time I was morose and uneasy, finding the beliefs of the literalists to be a mere caricature of religion, but the method and programme of liberal radical criticism to empty religion of its power to speak with authority and power. So I went back to the Bible – to the King James version which has created religious English and whose phrases and cadences are even built into the way we think and speak: you do not need to be specially religious to use in everyday life expressions such as 'some fell on stony ground', 'pass by on the other side' or even, 'Get thee behind me Satan!'

As I read the gospels, I came back to a strength of conviction which I thought I had lost once and for all with the faith of my childhood: I became convinced that the gospels are true in a sense which is so deep and undeniable as to be true absolutely. But I am no literalist, no fundamentalist. I have therefore tried to find one sentence with which to convey what I mean when I say that the gospel story is true. Here it is:

When we read the story of Jesus we find we are also reading our own story.

This book is a systematic unpacking of that one sentence; an attempt to understand in what precise form the story of Jesus is spiritually and psychologically inevitable. For, turning from the Bible to modern thought, I discovered a strange fact: Even the secular thinkers who have seemed to threaten to destroy Christianity have unwittingly lent support to it instead. Only the language varies. Take Freud. He was generally taken to have made out that Christian religion is a sort of delusion, sometimes wish-fulfilling and at other times frightening and horrific, based on the young child's fears of his father. In Freud's psychotherapeutic method, however, we find a treatment of psychological character-ization which greatly resembles key aspects of Christian spirit-uality. Our unconscious minds are full of all kinds of primitive conflicts, fostering memories and fears which make us neurotic in adult life: we must come to terms with these and understand them with the whole power of our intelligence and emotions if we are to be freed from the neurotic strangulation of our personality. This seemed to me to be like the biblical account of sin – even of such an unfashionable doctrine as Original Sin! – repentance and salvation. To borrow a couple of phrases from the Prayer Book: 'acknowledge and bewail our manifold sins and wickedness' and 'the burden of them is intolerable' – these expressions, suitably remythologized, seem to be exactly what Freud's method demands.

Jung, who broke with Freud, is even more closely tied to Christian spirituality and you will find that I lean heavily on his helpful insights in this book. Even the old sceptic Bertrand Russell claimed that the categories of Marxism have their exact counterparts in Christian theology. Freud, Jung and Marx – I have named three great systematizers whose systems are, from an inward, psychological viewpoint, remarkably similar to Christian spirituality. But other, non-systematic writers also reveal the influence of Christianity even when they wish most to deny it. Nietzsche's insistence on life at all costs is much like Christ's claim that he comes to bring life abundant. The Absurdism of Albert Camus is a powerful spiritual concept which had much in common

INTRODUCTION

with fourteenth-century mysticism's preoccupation with God's absence. Sociologists' talk of 'alienation' and 'anomie' reminds me of biblical talk of separation from God, hell and damnation.

Perhaps I was innocent to find all this came as a surprise. What, after all, should I have expected? The human mind is shaped by the culture in which it lives. The culture of Western Europe has been created by Christianity, glued on as it were, to remnants of classical and semitic understanding. It makes no more sense to ask whether Christianity is true than it does to ask whether our culture is true. This is the point: *If our culture has somehow been 'in the wrong' all these years, on what basis do we discover that it is in the wrong?* Any such basis which may be alleged is bound to be part of that culture also.

We speak a common language. This means our minds are of a particular shape. And Western culture is no mere supermarket of ideas in which, guided by the likes of Mr Don Cupitt, we can choose what we like from the shelves on the basis of 'a little of what you fancy does you good'. On the contrary, we find that our minds are shaped by the Christian religion. When we dig down into the depths of our human experience, we find the words of the Bible – and especially the story of Jesus – coming up to meet us. That biblical story is the text in which human psychology is most completely described. I blame myself for all that wasted time in which I somehow supposed that what Professor Refined-Mind said by way of interpretation of scripture is more important than scripture itself. But when I say that scripture is indeed the text most basic to our self-understanding, I am not supporting literalism. No, we must approach scripture as we would approach an icon radiant with spiritual power. As Eliot said, 'You are here to kneel where prayer has been valid.' And as we kneel in meditation we tease out the application of His story to ours.

This is what I have tried to do in *Being Saved* because it has seemed to me so necessary to discover a religious way of knowing that transcends both the glib reductionism of the liberals and the strident incredibilities of fundamentalism. There is one quotation which has encouraged me more than anything else outside the Bible. It is from *Culture and Value* by Wittgenstein: 'Christianity is not a doctrine, not, I mean, a theory about what has happened and what will happen to the human soul, but a description of something that actually takes place in human life. For "consciousness of sin" is a real event and so are despair and salvation through faith. Those who speak of such things (Bunyan for instance) are simply describing what has happened to them, whatever gloss anyone may want to put on it.'

Let it stand then as the motto of my book.

Tockwith 1985

Peter Mullen

I JESUS

1 | Introduction

The Christian faith begins and ends with Jesus. He is the Alpha and the Omega, as the Book of Revelation says. But how are we to understand the person and work of Jesus today? Tradition tells us that the truth about Jesus is good news. But what is this truth? What is this good news? The basic facts about the life and death of Jesus do not look like good news. They seem to describe the tragic history of a good man. What are these facts? Indeed, are there any facts or is the whole gospel story a hopeless amalgamation of half-truth and hearsay?

Even the most sceptical of the biblical historians and critics admits the fact that Jesus did at least exist. This existence is corroborated by non-biblical first-century writers such as Josephus. However, this corroboration is brief, saying little more than the fact that Jesus existed and leaving aside any detail of his life. Modern scholars have tried to reconstruct a very basic life of Jesus – more of a summary of his life – from the accounts in the four gospels. This summary is not intended as a substitute for the gospels as if what they say cannot be trusted. It simply presents a rudimentary account of events which may be regarded as so certain that no reasonable man could wish to doubt them.

Jesus, a Jew, lived during the governorship of Pontius Pilate in Palestine (AD 26–36); he was a teacher (a rabbi); he was put to death by the Roman authorities on suspicion of insurrection. There is no good news in this. There is little news of any kind in it. Was Jesus the son of the carpenter Joseph, then? The scholars say we

cannot know for sure. Was he guilty as charged by the Romans?
Perhaps. What kinds of things did he teach? For this we have only
the words of the gospel writers and they wrote thirty, forty or more
years after Jesus' death.

It all sounds most unsatisfactory. Who could possibly prefer the
findings of modern scholarship to the riches that are contained in
the New Testament stories? But it is the duty of the scholar not to
claim more than his researches are able to substantiate. This
frequently results in modern criticism being regarded as something
that is negative and sceptical, niggardly and mean-spirited about
a tradition that has sustained the spiritual lives of millions since
the end of the New Testament period. But this is a *limitation* rather
than an *intention* of modern scholarship. Happily, if we agree to use
together the techniques of historical investigation and literary
criticism, we can affirm with confidence much more about the sort
of person Jesus was.

We do this by taking together the gospels and any other works
we can discover which we believe to have immediate historical
relevance and, by close attention and comparison of the documents,
we try to reconstruct a coherent and consistent biographical sketch.
Much will have to be excluded as uncertain. There is no harm in
that. Mere credulity is neither virtue nor intellectual gift. Much
more will appear in the form of loose generalization rather than of
firm historical fact. That this is bound to be the case becomes clear
when we see that the gospels themselves are at odds on points of
detail. For instance Matthew, Mark and Luke say that Jesus was
crucified on the day before the Passover; John says the crucifixion
occurred on the Passover itself. Matthew puts the three temptations
in one order while Luke puts them in another. In John's account
of the resurrection, Mary Magdalene comes alone to the tomb; in
Matthew's account, she comes with 'the other Mary'. These
discrepancies – and there are many more of them – may not
individually be important in themselves, but at least they show us
that there are some questions of detail which we cannot ask of the
gospels. It is only to say something about the sort of documents they
are: not literal, historical accounts (as, say, 'Hansard' purports to
be), but documents produced by writers who considered they had
a more important task to perform than the bald reproduction of
detail. When Luke, in the Acts of the Apostles, tells us that there
was a cloud over the mount of the Ascension, he is not giving us a

weather report. This does not lessen the impact of his narrative. I say all this only so that we might not ask of the New Testament questions which the New Testament itself does not set out to answer.

But the higher critical techniques allow us to say a lot more about Jesus than these bare details. When we take the reported sayings of Jesus and examine them in the same way as we would examine the sayings of anyone else, a particular character begins to emerge. Narrative accounts, whether factual or fictional, can be studied in the same way and produce the same sorts of conclusions. I am not saying that the gospel accounts are fiction; only that, when we read them, the character of Jesus emerges in the same way that the character of any fictional hero emerges. And novelists for instance are careful not to let their characters act out of character – or else the novel does not ring true. An Elizabeth Bennett would never become a whore, nor a Mr D'Arcy an inveterate gambler. A careful reading of the gospels reveals the character Jesus as one who rings true. For example, once we have heard his parables of the Good Samaritan and the Prodigal Son, we can predict what his attitude will be towards the woman caught in adultery. Bearing all three episodes in mind, we might find that the parable about the Sheep and the Goats (the Last Judgment) presents more of a problem.

2 | Who are we talking about?

There is no direct access to the truth about the person of Jesus. This does not mean that there is no truth about Jesus. It means that any such truth as we might discover is mediated by some sort of interpretation. A Jewish Christian of the first century might readily regard Jesus as the Messiah. This is because he already has in his mind the living idea of messianic visitation as part of God's purpose and truth for his people. A Gentile Roman Christian of the same period would not find the notion of the Messiah so useful. This is because messianic visitation plays no part in the tradition which shapes his spiritual understanding. So it is simply naive and no use asking whether Jesus was *really* the Messiah, as if being the Messiah were an attribute that could cancel all cultural barriers. The fact is that every generation, including the generation of the gospel writers themselves, has always interpreted Jesus in the terms of its own patterns of thought and expectation.

Still in some quarters there is this naive assumption that we can find privileged access to the person and work of Jesus, his identity, his place in the history of redemption and so on without having to go through the channel of one sort of interpretation or another. This is a mistake. St John says Jesus was the Word, Logos, Rational Principle of God himself; Rudolf Bultmann says Jesus is to be discerned in his 'authentic existence'. In fact, both writers are borrowing the intellectual jargon of one age or another – the philosophical presuppositions which their particular traditions have bequeathed. It makes no more sense to ask whether Jesus was really the Word, or whether he was really authentic existence, than it makes sense to ask whether he was really the Messiah, the Son of man or the Second Adam. There is no privileged starting point which does not rely on human categories for an understanding of the person of Jesus. This does not mean we can know nothing; but it ought to give us a decent share of humility about the sort of knowledge we think we might claim.

Let us take one particular and rather extended interpretation of the person and purpose of Jesus – one which has much to be said for it – and notice how it is and can only be *one particular* interpretation to which there are alternatives:

> God made the world and all that there is. He made man perfect. But man sinned of his own free will and rebelled against God. God, knowing that sinful man cannot enjoy the company of his creator, knowing also that because of sin he has no power of himself to help himself, entered the created realm himself in the person of his son Jesus. As Jesus he was crucified, thus bearing the punishment due to man. Afterwards he rose again from the dead that those who believe in him and in what he has done might be saved.

This is a plain and a coherent interpretation of the person and work of Jesus. It is supported by at least one tradition of New Testament teaching. If you can accept it, there is a real sense in which you can call yourself a biblical Christian. But, before you can begin to accept this interpretation, there are certain philosophical and metaphysical preconditions to be met. You will have to believe that whole system of an all-powerful creator God who has a special concern for mankind; also that this God is a pure spirit who is able to incarnate himself in man (a presupposition itself based on the philosophical presupposition of dualism); that vicarious punishment is efficacious; that it is possible for one to be revived from the dead and so on. In short, in order to accept what we are frequently informed is 'the simple truth' about Jesus, we shall need first to become acquainted with a complete system of cosmology combined with morality'– a system, in fact, of quite astonishing sophistication. This is a far cry from the alleged 'simple gospel' and 'plain truth' which confuses the wisdom of the wise and which has no use for the complicated mythologies of speculation. On the contrary, this interpretation is rich in mythological and metaphysical borrowings from many ancient traditions in religion and philosophy. It is not, of course, invalidated by its borrowings, but its supporters must not pretend that such borrowings do not exist.

There have been, and continue to be, hundreds of more or less helpful interpretations of the person and significance of Jesus: Ancient and modern, Jewish and Gentile, Alexandrian and Antiochene, 'heretical' and 'orthodox', Catholic, Reformed, Dogmatic, Liberal, Existentialist, Positivist and so on through the whole gamut of philosophical and ideological preconceptions. It is not possible to say with certainty which interpretation is correct and which interpretations are misleading and false; anyone making this judgment should himself expect to be accused of bigotry and unfounded dogmatism. What we might, more profitably, do is to ask of any interpretation whether it both fits the facts as we understand them and whether it proves helpful to our general understanding of Jesus.

3 | His Teaching – One View

The gospels present the teaching of Jesus as something fresh and vital, confident and possessing authority: 'You have heard it said . . . but I say unto you.' There is great power in both the style and the content of his teaching. And he did not pull his punches when it came to identifying and condemning his sham-religious opponents who also happened to be the religious leaders of the day, the Pharisees and the scribes:

> Woe unto you scribes and Pharisees, hypocrites . . . blind guides . . . ye are like unto whited sepulchres which indeed appear beautiful outward, but are within full of dead men's bones and all uncleanness . . . ye serpents . . . generation of vipers, how can ye escape the damnation of hell?'

The question is whether Jesus really did round on the religious leaders of his day in this fashion. How can we know the answer? Well, to begin with, the gospels are comparatively short documents and yet they are crammed with denunciations of the scribes and Pharisees. In Mark's Gospel in particular, Jesus is presented as fighting a running battle with them throughout his ministry. At any moment they will turn up to criticize and to condemn:

> 'Why doth this man speak blasphemies. . . ?'
> 'How is it that he eateth and drinketh with publicans and sinners . . . ?'
> 'Why do they on the Sabbath day that which is not lawful . . . ?'

'took counsel how they might destroy him . . .'
'By the Prince of devils casteth he out devils . . .'
'Why walk not thy disciples according to the tradition of the
   elders . . . ?'

and so on.

The amount of coverage given by the gospel writers to Jesus'
sayings against the scribes and Pharisees shows that this was
thought to be one of the most crucial aspects of his teaching – the
way in which he contrasted what he wanted to teach with what
was being offered by the establishment. If we were to discount this
contrast and this opposition, it would become impossible to begin
even to say much about the teaching of Jesus at all. There is a
consistency about Jesus' attitude to the scribes and Pharisees
which it is difficult to ascribe to editorial gloss or to the particular
prejudices of a particular writer. Moreover, since all four gospels
record this consistent opposition, it becomes impossible to disre-
gard it if we are to believe anything at all about what the gospels
tell us.

From this we can conclude much about the meaning of Jesus'
teaching. The scribes and Pharisees were sanctimonious, sham-
religious, thinking well of themselves, 'whited sepulchres'. Jesus
tells them so again and again. In the light of this realization, what
are we to make then of say, Luke 15.7:

   I say unto you, that likewise joy shall be in heaven over one
   sinner that repenteth, more than over ninety and nine just
   persons, which need no repentance.

Who are the 'just persons' here? They are the scribes and Pharisees
whom Jesus is attacking with sarcastic wit. They thought they
were just. They kept the law. They were 'not as other men'. They
gave tithes of all they possessed. And yet, for all that, we know
that Jesus called them 'whited sepulchres', 'serpents', 'generation
of vipers' and so on. He could not have meant them to take him
literally, then, when he spoke of 'just persons' in his parable about
the lost sheep. The only alternative is that Jesus was speaking
sarcastically.

Perhaps we begin to see a context in which to set Jesus' teaching
and that, whatever he meant by what he said, he did not mean the
same sorts of things that the scribes meant. This has important

consequences, notably in the interpretation of the Sermon on the Mount. For instance, there is the saying in Matt. 5.27–28:

> Ye have heard that it was said by them of old time, Thou shalt not commit adultery: But I say unto you, That whosoever looketh on a woman to lust after her hath committed adultery with her already in his heart.

Now the Pharisees were nothing if not thorough; they insisted that the law be kept in all its details, to the last jot. That is the rationale behind their stupid accusation that Jesus' disciples were working when they rolled the ears of corn in their fingers on the Sabbath day. In this saying about adultery, Jesus is pointing out the absurdity which arises out of their self-satisfied legalism. He is issuing a *reductio ad absurdum* challenge to their sanctimonious 'thoroughness'. Of course adultery involves more than a physical act. Its essence lies in the lust which is also its origin. But if Jesus – the Jesus who is sarcastic about 'whited sepulchres', 'blind guides' and 'hypocrites' – had stood up and made that pronouncement about adultery and meant it literally, he would, on any character-reading that rings true himself have been indistinguishable from the falsely religious, moralizing Pharisee. Whereas, the intended meaning behind this saying is, I suggest, that we are *all* adulterous in one way or another. In the same way, a few verses earlier, he convinces us that we are all murderers because there are times when we are angry with our brother. Jesus was not trying to be a super-Pharisee, to set an impossibly high standard, to moralize in a governessy way, 'Now, now, don't look at that woman like that – that's adultery that is!', or 'Don't you be so angry my friend – that's murder you know!' Where would be the good news in that? What he was doing instead was using hyperbole and irony to indicate human frailty, something shared by all men, even the scribes and the Pharisees – though of course their blinded sight (and ours too if we are not careful) would never have allowed them to own up to such a quality.

The same attitude comes across in Matt. 18.21.

> Then Peter came to him, and said, Lord, how oft shall my brother sin against me, and I forgive him? till seven times? Jesus saith unto him, I say not unto thee, Until seven times; but until seventy times seven.

Jesus was not saying that we must do the impossible. After all, most of us would find it impossible to forgive our brother even seven times; many of us find it difficult to forgive at all. Once again, Jesus was using the method of irony to draw attention to the way that we all behave towards one another. And so? So it ill-behoves any of us to get on our high horse and to think ourselves just, to think ourselves into the role of the respectable Pharisee who imagined that he could achieve virtue by the agreement of his conduct with the right side of a catalogue of prohibitions.

These examples are indication that Jesus' moral teaching was entirely realistic. He knew the nature of man and he did not insist like some drab moralizer that man should overcome, somehow, his dark side. The Pharisaical fault is the refusal to acknowledge the dark side's existence. That is why their morality was unrealistic; it was not founded on the perception of man as he is, but on some prescription about how he ought to be. Jesus asked us to face our failings. Very well, we are lustful, we are angry with our brother, we find it hard to forgive – what then should we do? Not dwell on our failings but accept them for what they are and do something else. What else? The clue is in Luke 7.47:

> Wherefore, I say unto thee, Her sins which are many, are forgiven; for she loved much.

The stress is not on what we cannot help but on what we can help. According to Jesus, we should live our lives to the full:

> I am come that they might have life, and that they might have it more abundantly (John 10.10).

Whether many of the sayings in John's Gospel go back to Jesus himself has been the subject of much questioning; but the *spirit* of that verse from John accords exactly with the *spirit* of Jesus' teaching in other parts of the New Testament. It is the very opposite of an obsession with rules and taboos as the way to righteousness. It is supremely non-neurotic, unafraid; and it finds a powerful expression once again in the Sermon on the Mount:

> Take no thought for your life, what ye shall eat, or what ye shall drink; nor yet for your body, what ye shall put on. Is not the life more than meat, and the body than raiment . . . which of you by taking thought can add one cubit unto his stature? And why

take ye thought for raiment? Consider the lilies of the field, how they grow; they toil not, neither do they spin: And yet I say unto you, that even Solomon in all his glory was not arrayed like one of these (Matt. 6.25–29).

This is more like *Fröhliche Wissenschaft* than the Traditions of the Elders. But it is not instruction for irresponsibility, nor does it contain any contempt for the flesh – as if food, drink and clothing were not important. It is hyperbole again, and used in the attempt to persuade men and women not to waste their lives in fruitless anxiety. No wonder Jesus lost patience with the scribes when they began to quibble about the fact that his disciples did not go through the motions of ritual washing before they ate! (Matt. 15.2–6).

I have mentioned already the emphasis on forgiveness in the teaching of Jesus; it is interesting to see the basis of this doctrine. This is not legalism: you forgive me and I will forgive you. It is based on the perception that everyone from taxgatherers and outcasts to scribes and Pharisees stands in need to forgiveness. Before the woman caught in adultery, 'in the very act' he said.

He that is without sin among you, let him first cast a stone at her (John 8.7).

The lack of event following that saying would seem to show that the bystanders were aware of their own sinfulness already. Certainly sin was no new doctrine in the teaching of Jesus. But what was new was his perception that the universality of sin among men radically alters every man's status in the eye of every other man. If all are sinners then there really is no room for anyone to affect moral superiority over anyone else – exactly what the scribes and Pharisees did. We have all sinned. We are all in the same boat. The only reasonable policy in the face of universal sin is universal forgiveness. Jesus repeated this message again and again, and nowhere more emphatically than in the parable of the Unjust Servant (Matt. 18.23–35). There is no clash between justice and compassion here; if we really accept the fact of sin in our lives then compassion *is* justice. Forgiveness is freedom. The free man is no longer accused by 'the righteous', and, if he truly accepts forgiveness, he no longer accuses himself. The power of sin to destroy lives and to thwart purposeful activity derives from a system of morality that makes a calculus out of atonement; a

ritualized morality of the kind practised by the scribes always fails
to deal with the real consequences of sin (including psychological
consequences) and that is why it is bound to fail. In Jesus' teaching,
the doctrine of sin is a kind of metaphor which speaks allusively
about the nature of man. It is the doctrine of man's moral equality.

And what is sin itself? Not individual acts of naughtiness, but
the very thing that binds and restricts a man, hampers the purity
of his vision and diverts the singlemindedness of his will *because* he
wants to deny that he is a sinner and instead wishes to claim a
little virtuous space for himself. Like the Pharisee in the temple,
he uses the space to pass judgment on others: 'God I thank thee
that I am not as other men are, extortioners, unjust, adulterers, or
even as this publican' (Luke 18.11).

That smug utterance is a false perception of the nature of man.
And such a false perception is at the root of sin itself. It is an
untruth. A perverted vision of reality. And it is entirely self-
defeating for by insisting on his own sinlessness, the Pharisee
commits sin – 'in the very act', as it were. We find a similar theme
in the attitude of the Elder Brother in the parable of the Prodigal
Son (Luke 15.11–32) when he says,

> Lo these many years do I serve thee, neither transgressed I at
> any time thy commandment: and yet thou never gavest me a
> kid, that I might make merry with my friends (Luke 15.29).

He is protesting his own righteousness but, according to Jesus,
that is something which no one is entitled to do. And, once again,
it is the very act of protestation which reveals the sin. We are
acquainted with the Elder Brother's limitations, his sinful small-
mindedness just as he speaks those words to his father. An example
of the same thing in comparatively recent writing is the clear and
indubitable transmission of Mr Collin's odiousness in *Pride and
Prejudice* precisely through his protestations of loyalty and humility.
The profession of superior righteousness is exactly what makes us
dislike him. It is the moral stance of the Pharisee.

Jesus was more at home among the sinners and outcasts than
among the scribes simply because the former had a true perception
of human nature while the latter held one that was false. It is not
a case of Jesus being like some smug revivalist who deliberately
searches out those who inhabit what seem to him to be the most
squalid corners of depravity in order to bring them the whole

paraphernalia of moralizing; it is rather a case of his choosing company among those who *know* what they are rather than among those who only *pretend*. There are no chief sinners. Sin is a universal tarnish. But it remains true that the only people who cannot experience the forgiveness of sins, and the freedom which forgiveness brings, are those who do not see themselves as sinners. This 'seeing' must be from the heart of hearts; a glib and wordy ritual penance is no use at all. It is the basic perception and understanding of our nature and how we see ourselves which must change. Jesus cannot make friends with the scribes and Pharisees because, though they are outwardly religious, they have no understanding of that basic religious truth about the nature of man – that he is a sinner. Other men may be sinners of course; but 'God I thank thee that I am not as other men'. But you are! says Jesus. That we're not! say the self-righteous. And so there can be no companionship between them.

I have concentrated attention on the scribes and Pharisees because they play such a big part in the gospel accounts of the life and teaching of Jesus and it is through Jesus' attitude towards them that we approach the centre of his moral teaching. I am not trying to single out the scribes and Pharisees for special punishment. For the harshest words about the morality for which they stood, read not this chapter but the twenty-third chapter of St Matthew's Gospel. It is the Pharisaical attitude which stands for sin himself. How the Pharisees must have tormented themselves! You cannot imagine *them* as lilies of the field. But it was their own attitude which made them – as it will make us if we are not careful – anxious, backbiting and desperate.

The centre of Jesus' teaching is the freedom that derives from our seeing our human solidarity as forgiven sinners. Jesus set down no catalogue of rules and regulations for the moral life. He issued no revised Traditions of the Elders. He would surely have laughed at the pharisaical Guru-communes of our own day, filled as they are with taboos, proscriptions, food laws, self-congratulation and sectarian exclusiveness. For the most part, his own disciples carried on fishing. Sometimes Jesus did suggest that a man should change his life-style dramatically, but, as in the case of the rich ruler (Luke 18.18ff.) the suggestion was made within the context of an 'acted parable' and the conclusion to be drawn is general rather than specific.

The specific point is about money and this world's goods, another topic upon which Jesus had much to say. What he did not say was that the things of this world – money, houses, farms, land and so on – are evil; he did say that it is foolish to set our hearts on them. Consider the parable in Luke 12.15–21 about the rich farmer. When God says to him,

> Thou fool, this night shall thy soul be required of thee: then whose shall those things be which thou has provided?

God is not issuing a threat of punishment as if the man will be required to do penance after death for all his pleasure in this life. God is not saying that it is naughty to be wealthy and for that naughtiness there is a special punishment. Instead, Jesus meant us to understand that the man who sets his heart on material things has lost his soul already because,

> A man's life consisteth not in the abundance of the things which he possesseth (Luke 12.15).

It is significant that Luke follows this parable with the saying about the lilies of the field. A man's life does not *consist* in the things that he owns. What can this mean except the truth that it is the things we value which set a value on the quality of our lives? A man who sets out, like the man in the parable, to make money, well, he will be a man who makes money perhaps, that is how he will live and that is how he will have to die and be remembered by his inheritors – as a man who made money and that is all. The quality of his life – what the New Testament calls 'eternal life' – will be defined entirely according to the principles of money-making. Money will be the measure of the man's soul. The punishment for such a life is not dealt out after death by a heavy-handed Judge; it is itself the barrenness of soul which attends such a life while it is being lived. Better to be as one of the lilies of the field, as one of the fowls of the air.

Jesus is not like the Financial Adviser to the Diocesan Synod, laying down guidelines about the right and wrong uses of money; it is false and anachronistic to try and deduce Socialism or Capitalism from the teaching of Jesus. He was instead showing the place of wealth in the life of the soul, the value of worldly riches to spiritual progress, to real life. He did not value these things highly. True spirituality comes through a thankful acceptance of life itself and through an acceptance of the shared imperfection of our creatureliness. The heaven where moth and rust do not corrupt is the soul of the man who does not set his heart on the things that fade. 'Where your treasure is, there will your heart be also' is profound precisely because it describes perfectly the human heart. A heart set on corruptible treasures is corrupt. A heart set on 'eternal life' is alive.

The most striking aspect about the teachings of Jesus is that they are true in an unconditional way. They are not part of a system and they do not require the structured support of a system. For example, as a man of his time, Jesus believed in God who made the whole earth. As a devout Jew he also believed in the special status of the people of Israel. He looked forward to the Judgment and to the Messianic Banquet in heaven – his parables are full of it – as much as anyone else did. But Jesus' teachings are true to the experience of all men at all times, Jewish or Gentile, ancient or modern. Moreover, they are true for atheist and theist alike. This is because they are not limited to any particular metaphysical scheme. They are about the inward truths which man learns of his own soul. The truths which he cannot deny without going against his own experience. Like all truly original teachers, Jesus came stating the obvious in a fresh and original style. We know, as we have always known, that we are imperfect, sinners; but the teaching of Jesus on this topic is so startling that we can no longer evade the fact of our imperfection, no longer take comfort in the quiet respectability which earnestly identifies others as worse than ourselves. We know too that the quality of our life does not depend upon the shallow riches of material gain; but it is the stories about the moths and the rust and the pearl of great price which convince us even in our covetousness. It is the genius of Jesus' style that touches those parts of our being which moralizers cannot reach. We know that co-operation is better than attrition; but it is the irony, the twinkling hyperbole and paradox about a saying such as 'Love your enemies' which reminds us with force we are not able to resist. If I say that Jesus' teachings are psychologically true for atheist and theist alike, this is not through any aim to make Jesus out for a Death of God theologian. That too would be anachronistic. It is because I want to insist on the immediacy and the practical nature of these teachings. They speak directly, as they have always spoken, to the way we live now.

4 | His Life

The life of Jesus is not separable from the teaching, of course. But the life itself is part of the teaching. It is in the life of Jesus that we are to find the good news. It is a life we know little enough about and any attempt to reconstruct a biography of Jesus on the style of the nineteenth-century 'liberal lives' is bound to be a failure. We simply do not have enough information. If no biography is possible, we must be content with a biographical sketch. This sketch appears at the beginning of chapter 1. However, as a glance at the teaching has shown, it is possible to reconstruct something of Jesus' character; indeed his character is communicated with astonishing clarity wherever we open the gospels. And the gospels tell us not only how Jesus acted but also how he reacted to the events which forced themselves upon him. This too is part of his life.

If you read the Gospel of St Mark up to chapter sixteen verse eight, it appears to be a tragedy. It is the story of a good man's progressive alienation and final defeat. At first the crowds follow him everywhere so that he has to take a boat in order to find space for himself. Gradually the crowds, as crowds will, withdraw. His family and the people of his village turn very cool towards him (Matt. 13.57–58). The disciples run away when Jesus is arrested. He is betrayed by one of his close friends. One of his very best friends denies all knowledge of him. Finally, on the cross, he loses even the faith which had sustained him and there is the terrible cry, 'My God, My God, why hast thou forsaken me?' The tragic fate of a good man. Did he really utter that cry or is it a piece of editing by St Mark in order to concur with the opening words of Psalm 22? It does not matter, for we can be certain that in any case Jesus experienced dereliction.

Brutally summarized like that, the life of Jesus seems to be bad news rather than good news. Would it not have been far better if events could have been arranged so that his life and ministry had been an obvious triumph and his followers thus able to proclaim a tangible glory to the world? But that would have been exactly the sort of triumph which does not belong to religion. One more prince among princes would do nothing towards the enrichment of the human soul. Those who look for the King to be visibly the King only repeat Pilate's mistake in John 18.33. A mixture of political aspiration and idolatry.

But Jesus rose again from the dead; surely that was a visible testimony to his power? The trouble with a literal understanding of the resurrection is that it only makes sense, and *can only* make sense, if all the rest of the mythological-supernatural explanation of the world is accepted exactly as it stands. Perhaps it is true just as it stands. Perhaps the first-century middle eastern account of the origins and purpose of the universe and man cannot be improved upon. Perhaps there are angels and demons and whole-sale miracles and a bellicose God who requires the death of his son as a sacrifice for sin. (Though some might wish to conclude that even the God of the Old Testament who prevented Abraham from sacrificing his son is more morally advanced than this.) But if that first-century explanation is correct in all its prescientific and savage detail – with the resurrection thrown in as a happy ending – it is still powerless to touch the soul of man in the way that a spiritual understanding of Jesus' significance can do.

The story of Jesus is not a device which may be used by us to evade the notions of suffering and death, to pretend that everything will turn out all right in the end. That is not gospel; it is wishful-thinking; there is no reality in it. Jesus stands for the affirmation of man in and through his suffering and his death. The quasi-supernatural figure of Jesus as presented by much popular (perhaps there is more to that word than I guessed!) apologetics is about as real, and about as useful to genuine needs, as Marvelman or Batman. He is a caricature God dressed up as a man, able to lay down his life and take it up again as he pleases. This image is an

idol. Paradoxically, he can do anything – *except* free himself from
the constraints and definitions of ancient supernaturalism!

The real Jesus is a real man, or else the doctrine of the incarnation
is a sham. He suffers the loss and dereliction which we suffer,
including the loss of faith and meaning. Yet as we read the gospels
we see that his true spiritual glory is not diminished by the tragedy
of his life. The good news, then, is that as he suffered so we suffer
and as he is glorious – not 'behind' 'inside' or 'after' the suffering
but in and through it – so we are glorious too. He is truly the Son
of Man, representative man; and his representation shows us how
to live in the face of suffering and death. That is what Jesus does
for us. There is nothing else which he can do for us. He is the way
we shall all go whether we like it or not. The choice, the decision,
the meaning of turning to Christ, is simply one of whether we will
go the way as he taught it or turn aside from his teachings. The
choice is of whether to live and die like the Pharisees or like Jesus.

Some will ask where is the glory in a life of suffering that ends
in betrayal and death. In order to try and answer this, we must
first ask what form that glory could take. What kind of glory is it?
If we rule out the cartoon triumphalism of physical resurrections
and an audible Last Trump, where is the glory in the lives we are
obliged to lead? The truth is that life is what it is whatever we
might wish about it. We do suffer and we do die and there is no
denying these facts. The only glory that is possible, then, is in the
way we live in the face of their necessities – with our hearts set
upon the unhelpful treasures which moth and rust corrupt, or
instead upon that awareness of myself and my spiritual significance
which the New Testament calls the kingdom of God.

This is where the gospel story of the life of Jesus helps. The main
incidents of his life as there recorded have about them something
of the nature of sacraments; for under the literal telling there is
lasting psychological and spiritual meaning. To claim this is not
to dilute the message of the New Testament, to pawn some alleged
'objective' truth for an interpretation which is merely 'subjective'.
All so-called purely 'objective' events such as the miracles and the
resurrection can be redescribed in a variety of ways – indeed the
four Gospels have their own far from insignificant differences on
the issue of the resurrection alone; and if an event can be described
in more than one way, then the 'real' nature of that event becomes
a subject for debate, for a genuine exchange of views. The radical

theologian's intention is not to undermine the gospel, or somehow by contrivance of dubious scholarship to try to make Christianity seem implausible; on the contrary, his task and his purpose is to present the gospel in a language – a language of faith as well as a literal language – which his hearers will understand. There is, after all, nothing particularly innovative about this method; it was used by the New Testament writers themselves. Compare for instance the theological setting of John's Gospel with that of Matthew's, or the full-blown cosmic Christ mythology of Colossians with the Jewish background to Galatians.

Theologians have usually tried to speak the cultural language of their day even when this has meant a radical departure from the ways in which a previous generation presented the faith. The Early Fathers taught a christology which, in many places, would have been incomprehensible to St Mark. This is not to say that Christ became incomprehensible, but that the language by which Christ was taught and preached was revolutionized. This has not happened once but again and again. Theology in the West was entirely recast again in the Middle Ages after the rediscovery of Aristotle. The language of theologians does not simply follow slavishly the language of the epoch; sometimes it helps form the contemporary language – as the plays of Shakespeare helped form English. And at the Reformation, theological language and insights were specially creative. What happened then was not a return to the way in which the New Testament preachers understood and proclaimed Christ but a radical rediscovery of the gospel in terms that caught the imagination of the people of sixteenth-century Europe. In the eighteenth and then the nineteenth centuries, Christianity shared the new Romantic language of the age first in the preaching of Wesley and the other Evangelicals who appealed to emotions as well as to intellect and then in the asesthetics of the Anglocatholic Revival and Ritualism.

It should not seem so shocking then that twentieth-century Christianity reflects many of the predominant ideas of our own age. There may be such a thing as pure truth but, whatever that is, it never has been and never can be the same thing as the truth which men try to express in language. And any attempt to convey the truth in a language which is not that of the age and period is bound to end up in obfuscation and obscurantism. There is no reason to suspect that the language of our own day is any less adequate for the preacher's task than say the language of Aquinas or Luther. If Christ is part of the revelation in time of the timeless spiritual realities, then all ages will find an authentic way of speaking of him. In our own century we may suppose that this preaching will take account of new and genuine insights – what an earlier age would have called 'the movement of the Spirit' – such as analytical psychology and literary criticism. In the rest of this book I want to try to explore the relationship between the story of Jesus as recorded in the gospels and our own spiritual experiences. The story of Jesus is an old one, but the language we use to talk about our spirituality – indeed the language in which we experience our spirituality – owes much to the insights of the twentieth century.

II THE LIFE WITHIN

1 | Introduction

It is easy to become arrogant or snobbish about the spiritual life, insisting that it is a particular sort of thing which 'the best people' have like a good education or a liking for classical music. In fact everyone has a spiritual life of some kind or another; it is that part of life which is not limited by the ordinary necessities like eating and sleeping – though eating and sleeping themselves *can* become parts of a genuine spiritual attitude and design. Of all the people who have a spiritual life, some take another step and become conscious of their spiritual life. This encourages them to attend to their moods and feelings, to try to analyse and so understand what is happening to them and, if possible, to make progress in what they consider to be the right direction. This activity, this awareness of oneself as a spiritual being, may involve prayer and meditation and the reading of religious books. But, while spirituality can be adequately described within the categories and vocabulary of a religious system, it is not limited by any particular system.

In the field of literature for example, there are spiritual truths to be gleaned from Jane Austen and George Eliot as well as from the more 'specifically religious' books like *Pilgrim's Progress* and The *Imitation of Christ*. And it is not as if one kind of spiritual truth here is any the less important or shallower than another kind. There is no ghetto of religious or spiritual truth immune against all the brash assaults of secular literature any more than there is a world of spiritual music separated off from the rest. The reality of heaven may be glimpsed in Mozart's *Requiem*, but it is there also

in the 'profane' *Violin Concerto* of Alban Berg. Spiritual experience
is indivisible and in a class of its own (*sui generis*): all profound
shifts in consciousness and affection involve our spiritual nature.
This is true even when the spiritual experience is derived from
chemicals such as opium, alcohol or the recently fashionable LSD.
Anyone who doubts this should consider the havoc which these
drugs can cause to the spiritual life and to the general psychological
makeup of the individual. Not all spiritual experiences are good
then; but all deep movements of the soul are undoubtedly spiritual. Perhaps this is a contemporary way of understanding I
John. 4.1:

> Beloved, believe not every spirit, but try the spirits whether
> they are of God.

Arrogance in spiritual matters takes two main forms. First there
is the attitude of the secular sophisticate who regards all talk of
religion as some sort of primitive aberration returned to haunt the
thoroughly modern consciousness. This is not true secular man
but merely uninformed, prejudiced man who cannot or will not
listen to the voices of the tradition which has formed him. Some
fell on stony ground. Secondly there is the narrow-minded religious
enthusiast who has certainly experienced *something* but who then
proceeds to limit spiritual reality to his own language and experience. In our age, this type is, unfortunately, everywhere to be seen
cajoling, bribing, threatening his neighbours into an acceptance
of the spiritual facts of life exactly as he, with his own very limited
vision, sees them. This is religious bigotry and one of the worst
consequences of spiritual pride. It usually involves some sort of
caricature of the truth, some approximation condensed into parrot-
fashion responses and accusations couched in redemptorist
language of one kind or another. There are plenty of examples,
each one scarcely distinguishable from the next – except to
committed participants who always seem to see in the doctrines
and practices of those most like themselves the very image of all
that is false and perverse. And so the old religious sects are in
danger of becoming as bound by ideological prejudices as those
new religious sects – the varieties of Marxist theoreticians. Whereas
the truth is that spiritual experience and spiritual development is
not circumscribed by the conversion jargon of any one group. The

claim that it is so circumscribed and directed is akìn to the practice of idolatry.

However, close investigation leads to the conclusion that there is a similar psychological process in the individual whether the individual concerned is an Evangelical Christian, a Secular Mystic or a devotee of Analytical Psychology. Perhaps the old saying about man being made in the image of God is a way of describing this similarity. This process, this pattern of development, is, I believe, powerfully exhibited in the life of Jesus. And the fact that to some degree we all follow this pattern may throw much light on that phrase 'the imitation of Christ' as well as on other phrases like 'Son of Man' and 'the firstfruits', 'the Second Adam' and so on. I believe that one of the main reasons for the persistent freshness and appeal of the gospel story – just try the parables on any class of six year olds – is that we see Christ's story as our story. His way is the way we must go. Let us look at some details.

More than nine tenths of the gospels are concerned with the adult life of Jesus. Mark includes no birth narrative, no wise men, no flight into Egypt and no youthful visit to the temple like that found in the second chapter of Luke. These events are important in themselves however, but I think the best starting point for a study of Jesus' life begins where Mark begins it in his, the shortest of the gospel accounts. This is the story of John the Baptist and it is important for our understanding first of all because it reminds us that Jesus belonged to a living tradition of faith and religious development. John is a type of the Old Testament prophet. He leads a prophet's life, sparse, spartan, austere:

> Clothed with camel's hair and with a girdle of skin about his loins; and he did eat locusts and wild honey.

Jesus comes out of Nazareth and is baptized by John in the Jordan on the edge of the wilderness. There is no good reason to doubt that this happened just as Mark says, but the bold events are full of spiritual significance not for Jesus only but for anyone engaged in living the spiritual life.

First, I mentioned the fact that John stands in a particular tradition. Jesus' own spiritual awakening, of which this first chapter of Mark is an account, does not happen in a void; he becomes dramatically aware of the tradition of which he is an inheritor. This is true for us also. We do not begin to think about spiritual things in a vacuum but as we have been taught. And the symbols of the wilderness and the water are significant as well. Before a movement that generates spiritual progress in our lives we most often feel lost, aimless, wandering. And this is not confined to the emotions; we are anxious until our minds as well as our hearts can settle honestly upon an interpretation of our experience that is truly satisfying. This always requires a new movement, a new voice. But the heavenly voice cannot be heard except first we are bidden by a human voice. For Jesus this voice was John's. The necessity of John the Baptist is shown by Jesus' insistence (in Matthew's account) that John baptize him. We no longer live in the wilderness by the Jordan of course and the new movement, the voice which speaks to us in our spiritual wanderings, might be a new book or even a talk on the radio or the television.

But something happens to cause a new stirring, a stirring into life vigorous enough for us to call our past life a kind of death. For that is the symbolism of baptism, a death and a new life. It involves much more. First, as it did with Jesus, a submission. He consented to be baptized by John. We should not forget the radical passivity of baptism. That is a remarkable phrase in the Acts of the Apostles 'Repent and be baptized!' (Acts 2.38) for it is an injunction to combine the two elements – one active and the other passive – of a single act. These elements are complementary: to be baptized means to die in the old pattern of life; to repent means literally to change one's mind or, better still, to rethink. Secondly, baptism with its connotation of submersion as well as that of submission, signifies an encounter with unconscious forces, the depths. What happens next in the life of Jesus is a sign that that encounter with the unfathomable depths has taken place; for the ordinary descriptive language about his baptism suddenly, as it were, overflows into the ecstatic and paradoxical language of religious vision 'He saw the heavens opened, and the Spirit like a dove descending upon him. And there came a voice from heaven saying, "Thou art my beloved Son, in whom I am well pleased" ' (Mark. 1.10–11).

This is the language of conversion and annunciation. The experience is one of awakening and reorientation. Jesus is told who he is as he is baptized, where the giving of a name has traditionally taken place ever since. And the name is what signifies identity; it is the sign for the beginning of self-awareness, of self-consciousness.

Corresponding to the baptism of Jesus in our spiritual life are exactly those experiences of self-awareness, reorientation and of our own identity which herald a profound directional change. Some people can point back to a particular experience which occurred on a particular day and which they look upon as a conversion or an annunciation. In Jesus' story, the heavenly voice, the voice of God guarantees what is spoken by the earthly voice, that of John the Baptist. Jesus comes out of the deep to hear the voice from on high. The spiritual and psychological encounter with his own depths, symbolized by the water, is validated by the heavenly (archetypal) language of acceptance and the identity-conferring symbol of naming.

In our own annunciate moments something of the same occurs. Depth speaks to height and we know that in the active-passive combination of call and response we are changed. But we cannot adequately describe this change precisely, because it is effected by forces which have hitherto lain unconscious. So our most likely immediate response will border on the ecstatic and the poetic and nothing will be what it is but 'like' something else – the very language of poetry.

And there came a sound from heaven *as of* a rushing mighty wind . . . And there appeared unto them cloven tongues, *like as of* fire . . . (Acts 2.2–3)

And the Spirit *like* a dove descending upon him . . . (Mark 1.10)

What we say at these times is also likely to be couched in the historic language of religious experience because this is the way in which man has always tried to give expresson to the inexpressible while at the same time distancing himself (by the simile and the metaphor) from the numinous power of the experience. For we should not underestimate the great danger of being overwhelmed by such experiences. It is after all, 'a fearful thing to fall into the hands of the living God' (Heb. 10.31). That is the true function of religious language, to be 'like' to be 'as of' to be 'as it were' instead of literal. If it were literal, it could never communicate, and at the same time defend us from, the reality which it signifies. Religious, ritualistic, liturgical and poetical languages have always combined this double function, that of revealing *and* cloaking. The desire that religious language, including all talk about God and spiritual reality, should be literal and straightforward rests on a mistake, namely the misperception of spiritual realities as ordinary, everyday, measurable and definable contents of experience. A God we can define and identify through literal prose ceases to be God and becomes an idol.

Even the secular age in which we live reserves the use of religious language for those subjects which it still regards as mysterious. Principal among these is death. The so-called 'death bed visions' so well reported recently are full of religious poetry and symbolism about 'heaven' and 'gardens' and 'choirs', 'angels', 'bright lights' and so on. This is because when we are faced with a mystery – not simply an abstract puzzle but an experience of 'the depths' – we have no choice but to use the language that has always been set aside for that purpose. Indeed, the question is perhaps rather one of our being used *by* the language than of our own conscious manipulation of symbols.

2 | The Shadow

But the ecstasy of annunciation means nothing unless it is translated into ordered speech. That is what Jesus does next in the story which is recorded for us as the Temptations in the Wilderness. The most immediately striking aspect of this story is the manner of its beginning; Mark, Matthew and Luke record that it was 'the Spirit' who led Jesus into the wilderness to be tempted by the Devil (Mark 1.12; Matt. 4.1; Luke 4.1). Jesus was not lured into the desert by Satan himself; neither did he wander there aimlessly. He was driven into the wilderness by the Spirit – by the same agent who had just pronounced his annunciation – in order that he might suffer temptation. This says much about those two religious characters the Spirit and the Devil.

In the Old Testament, God's Spirit was usually pictured as the breath of God. In the creation myth of Genesis, God breathes into Adam and Adam becomes a living soul (Gen. 2.7). Later the prophets of Israel were inspired – the connotation of breath again – by the Spirit of God. In short, anything that had life was possessed by the Spirit. A full portion of the Spirit, such as enjoyed by the prophets, was regarded as a mark of God's favour. As for Satan, or the Devil, he was never construed as the embodiment of all evil and still less as a supernatural power opposite and equal to God himself. For that doctrine is but to leave the world of the Bible altogether and consult the doctrines of Manichaean Dualism, the Gnostic Mysteries of the first and second centuries AD and, of course, the later poetical works of Dante and Milton – to say nothing of the even more lurid portraits to be found in popular art and films of our own century.

In the Old Testament, Satan is, on the contrary, one of the sons of God. He presents himself at God's court in heaven and there is, for instance, a conversation about God's servant Job (Job 1.6). Satan has a particular task. He is a kind of witness for the prosecution, literally a devil's advocate, a fault-finder. It is his job to accuse. This is entirely consistent with and exactly what we should expect from the radical monotheism which defined the religion of Israel. The only spiritual power is God. All life and movement comes from him. The Devil is put in his proper place as one of the sons of God, a power created by God and not an independent spiritual authority by himself. Any other doctrine about the origin and person of the Devil is inconsistent with the doctrine of God's omnipotence. If God was not responsible for the creation of the Devil, then that responsibility must lie elsewhere – perhaps with the Devil himself. And that idea is intolerable to those who proclaim the sovereignty of God.

In fact, the gospel writers take over this doctrine of the Devil as one of God's sons or servants. The Devil acts in a collaboration of psychological opposition to the Spirit. The Spirit and the Devil are necessary elements in the further development of Jesus' religious awareness. There are varieties of opinions about what actually happened at the temptations in the wilderness. Some interpreters take a literal line and picture Satan as an actual character met by Jesus face to face. Others imagine that the story of the temptations is about something which took place in Jesus' mind, a tremendous struggle out of which he emerged victorious. Whichever interpretation is preferred, I think it is vital to establish one fact straight away: it must have been possible for Jesus to have given-in to the temptations or else the whole episode was a sham. Commentators of all shades of opinion affirm that the story of the temptations is meant to comfort us with the knowledge that, as we are tempted, so Jesus was tempted also. But if there was never any chance that he would lose that battle with the Tempter, then he certainly was not tempted *as we are tempted*. And that, of course, makes a pretence of the whole doctrine of the incarnation; for it presents us with a Jesus who was only under the appearance of a man. Essential for the doctrine of the atonement, as well as that of the incarnation, is the vision of Jesus as a real man among real men. The alternative, a divine being who is only acting the part of a man, is no better and just as impotent to save us as a score of the heavenly redeemers of first-century Gnosticism. Wesley's chocolate soldier – 'veiled in flesh the godhead see' – cannot save us.

From a psychological point of view, the sequence of baptism and temptations rings true. It is a well-attested experience that a 'spiritual high' is generally followed by a period of doubt and depression. So it is appropriate that, after that marvellously affirmative vision of Jesus coming up out of the Jordan, he should immediately endure a time of trial, a spiritual crisis. I believe that a helpful way of looking at this crisis is to see it as something which occurred within Jesus himself, to picture the Devil as an aspect of Jesus' consciousness. This is anathema to orthodoxy of course which strips off and strictly separates all suggestion of sin and the shadowy side of human nature from the person of Jesus. That is the psychological origin of all the myths and stories about the Devil as an independent spiritual power. And orthodoxy will have to pay – some say it is already paying – a stiff price for this separation in terms of a dramatic restoration of the balance in our own age. That Separated Devil, denied for so long, will have his day. Psychological equilibrium demands it. And the apocalyptic visions of our own time are all the evidence we need. But to claim, as I have claimed, that Jesus must have had it in him to give way to temptation implies that the shadow side of the personality existed in him too. To claim that it never existed in him is once again to imply that Jesus was not a man like us, and the doctrine of the incarnation is forfeit once more. In fact, we have other evidence of the shadowy side in the accounts of Jesus' life. There is, for instance, the issue of the withered fig-tree (Mark 11.14–20); there are Christ's words to Peter (immediately after he had called him the rock upon which the church would be built!) 'Get thee behind me, Satan' (Mark 8.33); there are the numerous incidents of verbal violence towards the scribes and Pharisees; there is the physical violence used at the cleansing of the temple (Luke 19.45–46); and supremely there are the words of dereliction from the cross (Mark 15.14). No 'gentle Jesus meek and mild' could ever have done the things which he did; no religious or secular authority would have gone to the trouble of hunting down, torturing and finally crucifying anyone so milky and watery as the Christ of sanctimonious devotion.

In fact the shadowy side, personified in the story of the temptations, as Satan or the Devil is necessary to the development of
Jesus' religious understanding and to the integration of his own
personality. The Devil provides an alternative programme for
Jesus to follow. It is the presentation of this flawed alternative
which enables Jesus to direct his thoughts aright. Where there is
no wrong, no evil possibility, there can be no meaningful moral
choice. Jesus, like us, could discover what was right only by setting
it alongside what was wrong. In the practical sense then, that
mercurial figure of Satan is a moral catalyst. He provides the raw
material for Jesus' decision. The impetus for that decision is
provided by the Spirit. Hence the collaboration of these characters
as the gospel writers imply and as we experience in our own
psychological make-up.

Of course the Shadow – I have borrowed this usage of the term
from Jung – in Jesus' case is a powerful character; this is just what
we should expect as we know that the light side of Jesus' character
was so strong. That which is most solid and substantial casts the
darkest shadow. This is only another way of saying that we can
fairly assume the temptations of Jesus to have been proportionate
to his virtue. Or else they were not significant temptations. It is
important for our spiritual and psychological interpretation of this
story to see exactly what Jesus did in his confrontation with the
Devil, that is with the dark side of his own nature. He took it very
seriously indeed. He faced up to it, acknowledged it as a real
possibility before finally transforming its suggestions into what
was good and right. There is much to be gained from a study of
this process.

First, let us imagine the new Christian. Perhaps he has turned
to Christianity after a long, private, internal struggle. Or, on the
other hand, he might have been helped and encouraged by friends
to make a public affirmation of his conversion. Inwardly and
psychologically for every Christian, this conversion is a representation of that story about Jesus' baptism in the Jordan and the
coming of the Holy Spirit to validate the event. It is likely to be an
occasion of joy, perhaps even of ecstasy; and then the convert
might wish to use the language of poetic affirmation, as the gospel
writers do, to express his feelings, to describe the release that he
feels. If his counsellors are wise, they will warn the convert that he
is in for a big let-down. When the emotion of the moment – no less

genuine for the fact that it is passing – wears off and the convert starts the return to his daily routine and obligations, he will be oppressed by doubts and misgivings. 'Perhaps I imagined it all?' 'What did I want to go and make a fool of myself for in front of all those people?' 'Nothing has *really* altered at all' and so on. Unwise counsellors sometimes try at this point to reintroduce some of the early experience in an attempt to bolster the faith of the new Christian. This is a mistake. It is not spiritual development but a kind of emotional addiction in which the origin and cause of the initial experience is forgotten in the misplaced desire to relive the experience.

True spiritual development usually follows a clearly identifiable pattern of progress. After the faith comes the doubt. After the 'high' of conversion comes the 'low' the 'honeymoon blues' or what you will. In other words, after the Jordan river, the wilderness. From the fact that this pattern is so regular and general, we may assume that it has much to do with a proper balance in the soul or psyche. The doubt and depression should be faced as the original exultation was faced. When it comes to spiritual progress, as opposed to mere bouts of quasi-religious excitement, feelings of pleasantness and unpleasantness are of very minor importance. What is begun at a religious conversion is a process of growing spiritual awareness and understanding – the older books call this 'sanctification' – which does not end until death, if indeed it ends then. It is the process of inner growth. And as with all growth and change, there is pain and insecurity. When the pain and the insecurity ceases it probably means we are spiritually dead. This is the meaning behind that great tale of Goethe's about Faust. Faust wants to grow spiritually. He knows that this will bring with it a certain amount of suffering, but he knows also that suffering can be borne for the sake of the insight and self-discovery that goes with it. He wants to progress spiritually forever. In his own particular encounter with the Devil, he is encouraged to doubt his resolve. One day, says Mephistopheles, you will have had enough of this spiritual progress. You will say, Stop! You will want to stay where you are, to have the quiet life. You will say 'Stay thou art so fair!' ('Verweile doch, du bist so schon!') On that day I shall have your soul.

In that necessary dejection of spirit that follows religious conversion, the Christian – like Christ in the wilderness – is being forced to confront himself, to look at himself with a ruthless honesty he has not known before and to make a beginning at the long process of psychological integration. To see himself as he is and not how he would wish to see himself. This corresponds to Christ's encounter with the Devil who, so far as his own soul is concerned, represents the real possibility of evil and failure. Jung has called it the encounter with the Shadow, the dark side of the personality which must be integrated into the whole if genuine progress is to be made. The new convert feels that there is something not quite right, almost unfair about the way he is being tempted: 'When I gave my life to Christ, I imagined I was rid of *those desires* for good!' No wonder doubt and depression ensue.

Three courses of action are then available, only one of which leads to a continuation of spiritual development. The first false trail goes the way of giving up in the face of discouragements. 'Ah well, it looks as if I'm not really any different after all. I might as well give up all pretence at being a Christian.' This is the mistake of believing that a Christian is someone who is all virtue; whereas in fact, Christians like everyone else are made up of virtue and vice, good desires and bad ones. The remedy for this particular despair is to remember the manner of your conversion in the first place. You were not saved *then* by your virtues but by grace; why should you imagine that the virtues which were powerless to help you earlier should somehow be of assistance now?

The second false trail leads to a denial of the dejection and, as I have said, this often goes along with spurious attempts to recapture the feelings which attended the original conversion. With the denial of the dejection comes, of course, a denial of the shadowy aspect. It is no wonder that so many of those enthusiastic religionists who identify spirituality with a kind of frothy exuberance and very visible joy should find devils turning up all over the place. The Devil (that which is no more than the shadowy aspect of us all) will be acknowledged for what he is; or else if he is denied and left unintegrated, he will appear in places where we do not expect him. And those who cast out devils from others should beware lest the real meaning of their action lies in the unconscious attempt to deny the place of the Devil in themselves.

The third and more promising trail is the one that leads to a calm acceptance of myself, my virtues and my faults, and which works slowly and patiently towards an understanding of the origin of my faults and towards a subtle reorientation of my personality so that gradually these come to exercise less power over me.

All these religious states apply equally to the man who thinks of himself as secular; it is only a case of terminological differences. The unconverted persists in sin, where sin is conceived not as individual acts of naughtiness but as a state which separates us from an awareness of God. The secular equivalent of sin is nothing other than a habitual way of perceiving myself falsely, where this false perception means that I do not develop as I should as a person. I might become neurotic, afraid of illness and death, insecure, discontented, always looking for something that seems always to elude me. It does not matter whether I choose to call this a state of sin or not – it is certainly not a state of grace! – the result is the same. I am hampered from living life to the full – that 'abundant life' of which Christ spoke. My false perception of myself is what is doing all the damage and it is closely connected with the Devil, the Shadow or, more prosaically, simply my faults. An object projects a shadow. And that is what we do when we identify annoying faults in others. This activity of projection is well-known to psychologists and spiritual directors; it is a device by which I am able to avoid facts about my own nature which I find unpleasant by discovering the same unpleasant features in someone else.

The issue is unaffected by whether the other person has these features or not. Superficially, I avoid pain by avoiding myself, faults and all; but I must then suffer the much worse agony of neurosis, of what arises out of this false perception of myself. And until I accept and integrate the shadow, the door is closed against spiritual progress of any kind; if we do not like the religious connotation of the words 'spiritual progress' then 'self-knowledge' can be substituted for them. The key to understanding and doing something about this problem is to look at the shadow itself – the Devil facing Christ in the wilderness again. In other words, look at the particular projections, the particular shadow which we are casting. Ask ourselves, 'what are the features that I find so intolerable about so and so?' The odds are that these are the very features which we shall find within ourselves.

The word 'acceptance' becomes crucial here. The encounter with the Shadow, like all archetypal experiences of crisis, is most delicate from the psychological point of view and great care must be taken over its handling or much harm can follow. Revivalist attempts to convince people of their sins do little good. This is because the sinner knows already in his unconscious mind that he is a sinner. A sudden eruption, provoked from outside, of that knowledge into consciousness generally leads only to extravagant and disordered behaviour and to an even more strenuous projection of the Shadow. I have already mentioned the enthusiast's preoccupation with *other folks*' sins, with devils, demons and the like. These are simply the marks of projection. However, there is such a thing as a word in season, and it may be that a sermon, a talk or even just a word or a glance from someone else proves to be the final stepping-stone to the shore of self-discovery. When this happens we may assume that it is a more or less happy accident, since the preacher or speaker is hardly likely to possess privileged insight into the psychological and spiritual development of everyone he addresses. In fact, these chance reminders, these experiences that awaken religious consciousness (self-awareness) are generally most effective when they turn out to be just that – chance.

But there is also the view that these chance reminders are not really chance at all. When the external world seems to reflect something of our inner experience, Jung describes what is happening as an incidence of synchronicity – a significant coincidence. By this theory the unity of outer and inner worlds is proclaimed. Jung gives many examples arising out of his clinical practice. Biblical instances would include the Star of Bethlehem as synchronous with the birth of the Christ-child and the rending of the veil of the temple at the crucifixion. Synchronistic phenomena are like visual aids or acted parables. We might expect, and indeed we find, many examples in the poetry of nature and romance. One of the most telling is from Wordsworth's *The Prelude* in which he tells how he was made to shudder by the glimpse over the lake at night of a huge peak:

> . . . a huge cliff
> As if with voluntary power instinct
> Uprear'd its head. I struck and struck again,
> And growing still in stature, the huge cliff
> Rose up between me and the star, and still
> With measured motion, like a living thing,
> Strode after me.

Well, of course, it did no such thing. But that was how it felt to the poet. The external mountain was terrible because it coincided with an inner state. We can all point to similar experiences, if not with mountains with other aspects of the natural scene or upon hearing a certain piece of music and so on. The connexion between outer and inner phenomena is not causal; the cliff is not frightening in itself yet Wordsworth's anxiety might not have been awoken if he had not seen it. The anxiety was there all the same. The cliff was there too of course. On the doctrine of synchronicity they together make one complete and significant event which is a unity of object and psychic sensation.

The experiences which result from these combinations are among the deepest and the most memorable known to man. They may be referred to as archetypal experiences and they are powerful in bringing about change and spiritual development. Again we expect and we find that religious literature is full of accounts of visions and out of the ordinary experiences of this kind. They generally mark a period of crisis and transition in the life of the person who experiences them. We think of Jacob's ladder, of Moses and the burning bush, of Isaiah in the temple 'in the year that King Uzziah died', of Saul on the Damascus road. It follows that any attempt to promote or manufacture these experiences is a most dangerous occupation and one of which the preacher or spiritual counsellor or psychotherapist should beware. The appropriate unconscious development and maturing must first take place before consciousness can be significantly moved. Think of Saul on that Damascus Road again: he must have known, as an educated man, the Christian proclamation inside out and back to front; and yet he had to wait for the moment when outward events coincided with inward development.

There is another sense in which it is dangerous to try and hasten archetypal experiences of the conversion type, and that concerns the negativity and destructiveness of a certain kind of preaching. It is not at all helpful – certainly it is not good news – to tell a man he is a sinner. This is the sort of moralizing for which the scribes and Pharisees were famous. Besides, we are not saved by turning from sin and becoming good; we are saved by facing up to the sin and by acknowledging it as our own. Or, in another terminology which amounts to the same thing, we become more whole, better integrated, not by denying, projecting, casting out the Shadow but by accepting its existence as an ineradicable aspect of our nature and personality. In language free from the jargon of either Christian spirituality or analytical psychology, I mean to say this is nothing other than a true perspective about ourselves, our strengths and our weaknesses.

The integration of the Shadow is a gradual work requiring much gentleness and humour for it requires that we acknowledge our faults without allowing ourselves to become emotionally and morally paralysed by them. That such paralysis can and does occur is the testimony of our religious tradition which has always known that 'the burden of them is intolerable' (General Confession at the Holy Communion, 1662). And even our faults must be seen in perspective. There is hubris in claiming that we are the chiefest of sinners and too much attention to our failings and weaknesses can be a kind of inverted spiritual pride. This is because a morbid introspection forces us to focus upon ourselves as if we were the centre and the most important creatures in the universe. This is not a sense of perspective but a lack of it.

We should not overlook the positive function of the Shadow. It is the origin of moral choice and a source of spiritual or psychological energy. In that story of the temptations, it is the Shadow who raises the important questions about the nature of Jesus' calling and identity: 'If thou be the Son of God' is the twice asked question (Matt. 4.3, 6). The dark side of our nature is similarly capable of originating ideas; what we should notice is that ideas formed by the Shadow are generally disordered, caricatures of the full blossoming which is the real goal of spiritual development. So in the temptations the function of the Son of God is regarded as the performance of a few conjuring tricks: 'Command that these stones be made bread'; 'Cast thyself down'. As if the definition of divinity were to consist in such showbusiness as these! But Jesus never simply rejects the Shadow's inspiration; he transforms, completes and reorientates it: 'Man shall not live by bread *alone*'; 'Thou shalt not tempt the Lord thy God'; 'Thou shalt worship the Lord thy God and him only shalt thou serve'. Neither bread nor worship is rejected, but it is in Jesus' answers correctly relocated in the complete perspective.

The man who successfully integrates the dark side of his nature is likely to be the sort of man who has a cheerful awareness of his faults and weaknesses. He perceives their emergence in all the ordinary dealings of every day and he makes appropriate adjust-

ments. He is neither morally paralysed nor under the false appre-
hension that he is capable of more good than a limited amount.
He sees himself neither as chief of sinners nor as angel of light. He
knows his limitations. He avoids projection. Paradoxically, it is
the knowledge of our limitations which enables us gradually to
begin to transcend them. But the process of sanctification (or in a
less overtly 'religious' language) of psychological integration and
self-knowledge lasts a lifetime. There are dozens of incidents in the
gospels where Jesus casts out devils. This was after all only what
any competent teacher was expected to be able to do in first-
century Palestine. Even the Pharisees were in the business of
casting out demons (Matt 12.27). But the psychological impli-
cations are of interest because the frequent reappearance of the
devils shows that the Shadow is never completely cast out. It is
always disordered, as the evil spirits in the gospel stories are
sometimes deaf and dumb, at other times violent and again
'unclean'. But the Shadow itself becomes more sophisticated and
its challenge to wholeness becomes more formidable, as we discover
more about the dark side, the dark side also increases in knowledge.

And devils also came out of many, crying out, and saying,
Though art Christ the Son of God (Luke 4.41).

The scribes and Pharisees did not know he was God's son, but the
devils knew it! By this parable we learn that the struggle for
wholeness develops new complexities as it goes on. Always, the
ambiguous nature of the Shadow should be remembered. It is,
unacknowledged, a danger and a barrier to spiritual progress.
Accepted as an ineradicable aspect, it is of much use. Just as the
Devil is not God, nor any sort of rival God, but a created aspect of
the divine economy, so the Shadow is not independent, not
autonomous but exists only as a part of the whole edifice of the
personality. He is like one of the characters – even if not our
favourite character – in the play. He is also God's son. The
alternative to this analysis can only be that the Devil or Shadow
is an independent force for whom God is not responsible. This
conclusion is intolerable for Christian monotheism. And, within
our own experience of ourselves, we know that the Shadow is real.
We know also that he is only a part of our being and that he is
finally subject to the total organization of the whole personality.
In mythological-religious terms again, God will eventually 'beat

down Satan under our feet' as the Litany says. That is where he can do no more harm, but it still guarantees him his place.

3 | The Woman

The world of religious imagery is full of opposites: heaven and hell; life and death; angels and devils; Christ and Satan (the two sons of the one God); light and darkness and so on. The Bible begins with an account of those terrestial opposites man and woman. All these images have psychological correlation. The 'objectivity' of the images is mirrored in the 'subjectivity' of the soul or mind. Any stress on one aspect 'objective' or 'subjective' to the exclusion of the other is therefore a misapprehension of the reality which is in fact an 'objective-subjective' continuum. It is this link, this continuum, which ensures that observation and contemplation of the images always falls back into meditative silence and the prayer through which we try to see the significance of the images for ourselves; and which also works the other way about, as when introspection and contemplation spill out into both action and art. In the process of psychological development, there is a particular pair of images which is of similar importance to that of the Shadow. These are the male-female aspects, or, as Jung calls them, the anima and the animus. Events in the life of Jesus as recorded in the gospels bring out the significance of this pair, of this conjunction of opposites.

Women feature prominently in the life of Jesus. This is extraordinary in itself given the low status of women in first-century middle-eastern life, and especially in the religious life of the time which was essentially a male prerogative. Women were among his companions and it must be said that, in terms of quality of discipleship, they were at least as good as the men; better than the men if the gospel accounts of their presence at the crucifixion (when the twelve had deserted him) are accurate (Mark 15.40; Matt. 27.55–56). And women are present in every account of the empty tomb. The old and controversial questions about Jesus' sexual relationships with women – whether, for instance he ever married – are not worth going into for the very good reason that no clue of any kind can be inferred from the gospels themselves. But the gospels are unanimous in the affirmation that, in the male-dominated world of the first century, Jesus had much to do with women.

From a spiritual and psychological point of view, it is significant that women were so prominent at key archetypal stages in Jesus' life: the nativity of course but also the death, burial and resurrection. The significance is in the relationship between the events themselves and the psychological experiences which they mirror in every human life. For birth, suffering, death and rebirth are psychological events as well as physical occurrences. In the religious language they are events which concern the soul. The old word for soul is anima, a feminine noun, and the physical correspondence to the anima within is the woman. The hero's companion is a physical representation, a personification, of his soul. The world's literature is full of archetypal couples from Dante and Beatrice through Faust and Gretchen, Abelard and Heloise to Tristan and Isolde. In Jung's language, the mythological personification of the anima in all these stories represents truth not merely about the objective woman but about the soul of man; and the reciprocal personification of the objective man (animus) speaks about the inwardness of the woman.

Just as we are made up of the opposites light and dark, ego and Shadow, so each one of us has consciousness and the unconscious, masculine and feminine aspects of our character. And, as with the ego and the Shadow, the task once again is one of balance and integration of these aspects; in the case of the anima, however, this is more difficult because we are dealing with a conjunction of a conscious aspect with one that is unconscious. Whereas the Shadow is mainly on the surface of consciousness and can therefore be identified reasonably quickly, the anima belongs to the unconscious and consequently its appearance is more subtle. Moreover, many people reject even the idea of the anima, imagining it to have

connotations of effeminacy, as if it were being suggested that men
are basically homosexual and women 'manly'. In fact nothing of
the kind is being suggested. The social and biological history of
man has guaranteed that certain masculine traits predominate;
finding a mate, hunting, defending a home against marauders
require a certain sort of decisiveness, even of ruthlessness. But
the gentler qualities still exist in the male and it is crucial
for psychological integration that these are acknowledged and
accommodated. The similar recognition of the animus, 'the male
within' is necessary to the wholeness of the woman. Because both
anima and animus aspects are unconscious, a certain amount of
reading the signs, of symbolic interpretation, is required.

A man's relationship with his anima, how far he has succeeded
in integrating this aspect, can be inferred from his relationships
with women. This is where Jesus' acceptance of women tells us so
much about his own spiritual progress and also sets out a pattern
of psychological maturity for all men. Jesus' forgiving, accommo-
dating attitude towards the women he met testifies to the integration of his personality in all its aspects; for the real, outward
women of the gospel stories also represent the inward characterization of the whole personality. Imaginative literature, and
especially the classics, contain many examples in which there is a
spoiled relationship between the man and the woman. This usually
signifies a disruption in the psychological or spiritual life of the
inner man. For instance, when Faust kills Gretchen that is where
he loses, temporarily, his own soul. In Dostoevsky's *The Brothers
Karamazov*, the cold, sceptical Ivan is never accorded the Russian
familiar name Vanya – the reciprocal feminine ending. This
signifies his rejection of the feminine aspect, of all that is warm,
gentle and intuitive. We may assume that Dostoevsky knew what
he was doing; great writers were aware of the nature of man's
psychology long before Jung gave us a quasi-clinical language with
which to express it. Because the anima is primarily an unconscious
phenomenon, we rely upon the mythopoeic character of certain
sorts of literature for much of our information about it. We can
also learn from dreams which are themselves a pictorialization of
unconscious events, and from the male-female attachments (or the
lack of them) in everyday life.

The first significant encounter with the anima is in the child's
relationship with his mother. To begin with this is a relationship

overwhelmingly one-sided in its pattern of dominance because, of course, the child is entirely dependent upon his mother. Gradually the ties of dependence are loosened and the child develops as a person in his own right – though this process can be hampered by an over-protective mother. Her effect is to keep the child unconscious of a world that exists apart from herself. Add an 's' to mother and you get smother. The emergence of psychological independence is pictured in the story of Jesus in at least two sections of the gospel: the first is the episode of his visit to the temple at the age of twelve; the second is the story of the water into wine. In the first, there is a clash between Jesus and his mother:

> And when they saw him, they were amazed: and his mother said unto him, Son, why hast thou thus dealt with us? behold thy father and I have sought thee sorrowing. And he said unto them, How is it that ye sought me? wist ye not that I must be about my father's business? (Luke 2.48–49).

His father's business and his own business are the same thing. The young man affirms his independence.

In the story of the water into wine, Jesus speaks abruptly to his mother. C. K. Barrett says the words 'draw a sharp line between Jesus and his mother' and he reminds us that 'what have I to do with thee?' is the same question as that put to Jesus by the demons (John 2.1–11). The fact that this was the first miracle that he wrought in Cana of Galilee emphasizes the beginning of Jesus' independence, of which the famous story is a kind of epiphany. It is no mere coincidence that these gospels from Luke and John are appointed to be read on the First and Second Sundays after the Epiphany.

Independence from the early, childish attachment to the anima is the beginning of the way to a mature perception of her. The aiteological tales of the Old Testament tell us that 'a man shall leave his father and his mother and shall cleave unto his wife: and they shall be one flesh' (Gen. 2.24). The discovery of mature relationships with 'objective' women corresponds to the parallel discovery of the 'subjective' woman, the anima. But the anima itself is not a static or changeless identity; as a living aspect of the personality it changes and develops through recognizable stages. Because this development is unconscious and within, it is best traced by a study of the various projections of the anima on to the external world. Such a study reveals a remarkable consistency in the order in which these stages follow one another.

The first stage usually takes the form of a more or less physical and erotic attachment and presents itself in art and literature among all the stories of the Temptress and the Siren. Eve in the Bible represents this stage as do the Sirens in the story of Ulysses' voyage, the Lorelei in German Romanticism, Gretchen in the first part of Goethe's *Faust* and so on. This primitive personification of the anima is seductive and dangerous. Eve attracts Adam but the attraction leads to tragedy. The Sirens lure the sailors on to the rocks. Why is this so? First, it should be said that this interpretation is meant as no slight to empirical women; man's downfall is not 'all woman's fault' but a result of mistaking an immature development of his own soul for the final perfection to which the whole personality aspires. The first encounter with the anima beyond childhood is an experience of overwhelming power. No wonder literature is full of judgments like 'lost his head'. The word 'fell' in 'fell in love' is very revealing when you think of the account in Genesis chapter 3. Like the appearance of the Shadow, the encounter with the anima is an experience which once again confers identity upon the young man. In the external world of relationships, he learns more about himself, who he is, through the process of getting to know his girlfriend. Inwardly there takes place at the same time a corresponding encounter with the unconscious, with the woman within. It is this double aspect of the meeting which makes it such an earth-shaking event in the young man's life; consciousness of the attractive power of the opposite sex coincides with the startling dawn of self-consciousness of his own eroticism. This stage represents another sort of annunciation and it should not be reviled or underestimated. The writer of the Genesis story knew that it coincided with the acquisition of knowledge:

> And the Lord God said, Behold the man is become as one of us, to know good and evil (Gen. 3.22).

It is interesting to note at this point that the Hebrew word for 'know' is the same as the word used to refer to sexual intercourse. This usage is found in many places in the Bible: 'And Cain knew his wife; and she conceived . . .' (Gen. 4.17). See also Genesis 4.1;

38.26; Judg. 11.39; 19.25; I Kings 1.4 and Matt. 1.25). All of life's
great or archetypal events yield knowledge about the world in
which man has to make his way, and they also have an impact on
the soul's pilgrimage of self-discovery and integration. The Adam-
Eve story replicates itself in the pyschological life of us all. There
is no avoiding it. The task is to learn from the various stages and
to use each in preparation for the next. The loss of innocence as
described in the Adam and Eve story is necessary to the emergence
of moral responsibility; there can be no choosing to do right until
we are aware of the difference between good and evil. Adam and
Eve are not less but more mature after the Fall. Before this they
were like the childish irresponsible Eloi in H. G. Well's *The Time
Machine*. And it is an equally childish and immature religious
consciousness which regrets the Fall as an event that spoiled
everything; for the Fall is necessary before the ascent and, in a
primitive sense, it prefigures the related though distant psychological progression of death and resurrection. The first is necessary
if the second is ever to take place. Man without the knowledge of
good and evil is not whole man. That act of disobedience in the
third chapter of Genesis certainly led to a curse but it led also,
indirectly, to a blessing marvellously evoked by Paul in the words,
'For as in Adam all die, even so in Christ shall all be made alive'
(I Cor. 15.22). The desire to avoid the psychological reality of the
Fall leads to a view of man which is merely coy, which is reflected
in the sentimental attitude of the Victorians and the Edwardians
towards the ideal of childhood – not to mention their loathing of
Sigmund Freud – and the naive evasions of *Peter Pan*. It is worth
reflecting on all that section about the boy who loses his Shadow.

'The Fall', 'Falling in Love' and this first descent into the
unconscious are related in terms of experience as well as linguisti-
cally. We begin our progress with a fall and this is as necessary to
what follows as the seed's burial in the ground is to its eventual
flowering.

First encounters with the anima can be frightening and appear
very negative in character. This is not surprising because every
archetypal character within the whole personality has its own dark
side. The stark presentation of the dark anima is seen in literature
and art in the characterization of witches like Circe and the Queen
of the Night from Die *Zauberflöte*. But even the witch cannot help
doing good though she only wishes to do evil. The Queen of the

Night is full of wicked desires and of Vengeance ('Der Hölle Rache Kocht in meinem Herzen') but it is she who also indicates to Tamino the way he must go if he is to discover the woman he loves. This is another example of the two-sidedness that is the nature of psychological contents. There is darkness in the Devil, but he is also called Lucifer, the bringer of light. So the witches also have their good uses.

The danger that is present in all the stories of a man's early encounter with the anima is inwardly located in the possibility that he may become fixated at one stage of his development, trapped as it were like sailors on Circe's island. However, as Ulysses knew, it is necessary to hear the voices of the Sirens; in other words, this particular stage, with all its delights and its dangers, must be negotiated on the way to the integration of the personality. But the problem is one of fixation or of being repressed to the early stage. This is what prevents progress. The man who is actually repressed to this phase is a familiar, if sorry figure – the forty year old who cannot free himself from a psychologically dissipating series of immature romantic attachments to young women. No doubt he really is in love with them; but his condition also speaks of his halted personal development and his nostalgic, even narcissistic, desire for a stage that is retrogressive. Goethe was like this. No wonder that he could not find the emotional maturity necessary for the completion of *Faust* until he was in his eighties! These attachments are not so much the search for a lost youth as a failure of the courage needed to move from one stage to another, from the known to the unknown in aspects of our inward life. And the desire for young mistresses is only another variation of the craving for an illusory security and comfort every bit as damagingly immature as the desire for so-called lost innocence. It is like remaining tied to the apron strings as the proverb has it.

As we have seen, when a man is able to accept his Shadow side and to begin to integrate it he makes psychological or spiritual progress and the archetype of the Shadow itself develops and matures. This is also what happens in the case of the anima which, if unrepressed, alters its representation over the years. From mother and then nymph, temptress or siren, the anima becomes companion. This is a stage which we see clearly in the life of Jesus. He is constantly among women who befriend him and whose friendship in the end has more stamina than that of the male

disciples. The companion stage represents a greater maturity as
the related function is no longer domination as in the case of the
mother nor enchantment by the erotic power of the seductress.
Though we should not be impeded by a coy attitude towards the
Gospels from seeing evidence of the temptress – siren stage in
Jesus' encounters with women. There is the episode of the Woman
of Samaria (John 4.9) and that of the woman caught in adultery
'in the very act' (John 8.4) which, though among other passages
also of doubtful authenticity in the Fourth Gospel, is generally
regarded as in keeping with Jesus' attitude towards sins of this
type and his compassion for the sinner. This certainly contrasts
with the attitude of the scribes and Pharisees whom we may
suppose to be so threatened by the anima that they insisted
vigorously on the death penalty for acts of adultery. Misogyny as
well as infatuation reveals in man a perverse rejection of his own
feminine aspect. Eroticism, penitence and pardon all find their
part in another gospel story about Jesus' relationship with a
woman: the Mary of John 12.3 who may have been the same
person referred to in Luke 7.37–39 and in Mark 14.3–9. And the
account in Luke 8.2 where Mary Magdalene is purged of the seven
devils also represents a purification of the anima leading to the
development of the next stage in which she becomes the companion.
The forgiveness and compassion which Jesus shows towards
'objective' women who are sinners – fleshly sinners in particular –
is balanced by a 'subjective' psychological or spiritual truth about
Jesus himself: his own success in the integration of the anima, the
recognition and acceptance of the feminine aspect. Compare once
again the consistently opposite and negative attitude of the scribes.

In discussing the Shadow, I tried to expose the false and
unhelpful piety which refuses to acknowledge the existence of this
archetype in the person of Jesus. If he had no Shadow, he was not
a real man and certainly not the representative man of Christian
tradition. The same is true in the case of the anima. Jesus was
obliged to go through the same adjustments and trials that we go
through in the integration of our psychological contents. If this
were not true, then Jesus would be quite useless as saviour and
redeemer. A representative man who manages somehow to evade
all the normal human difficulties is simply not representative man
but a superhero of gnostic invention or of science fiction. No
criticism of Jesus' person, psychology or morals is intended by

imputing to him the stresses and problems endured by all men at all times; in fact a genuine respect and admiration (both of which must come before worship and commitment) becomes possible only when Jesus is given the credit for having lived through and overcome problems of this sort. The alternative is that the incarnation was a sham.

There are two more personifications of the anima in its stages of development. The first of these is wisdom which in the Greek is given a feminine name Sophia. In the Old Testament and Apocryphal literature, an interesting balance is preserved between the 'masculine' intellectual struggle for the 'feminine' reward of Sophia. The search for wisdom is frequently portrayed as a sort of love affair which is a passion; perseverance and devotion play their parts along with all the other elements. This also shows that in the development of the anima – as in the development of all the archetypes – the early personifications are never entirely cast out or overruled; something of their essence persists though the original force of their presence is subtly assimilated and redirected. The compassionate wisdom characteristic of Jesus' teaching shows that this personification of the anima was integrated into his personality. And there exists a projection of wisdom and privileged insight in the person of Pilate's wife:

Have thou nothing to do with that just man: for I have suffered many things this day in a dream because of him (Matt. 27.19).

Pilate's wife has the real understanding of who Jesus is, 'that just man'. So does the woman with the precious ointment. She knows Jesus' purpose and destiny as she 'is come beforehand to anoint my body to the burying' (Mark. 14.8). But the Twelve had not such insight. Supremely in the New Testament wisdom is represented by the Virgin Mary. She it is who speaks the message of the Sermon on the Mount in the words of the Magnificat (Luke 1.46–55) where similar ethical contrasts are drawn to those which appear in Matthew 5 and indeed which foreshadow Jesus' familiar teaching method in the elevation of those qualities which 'the world' regards as lowly.

The final personification of the anima is virtue and once again this is seen supremely in the Virgin Mary his mother but also in the devotion of the women who follow him to Calvary and who prepare his body for burial. The Virgin herself is the key figure in this rôle for, as Christ is the Second Adam, she is the second Eve. The first Eve – the original personification of the anima – is a sinner, flawed, imperfect, the temptress, the cause of man's downfall; the Second Eve – the final personification of the feminine principle – is immaculate, sinless, the God-bearer, the earthly origin of man's redemption. It cannot be stressed too much that the archetype of the anima is one; there are different aspects but an essential unity. Or else Mary would be no more related to the real woman than Christ, in those docetic perversions which pass themselves off as incarnational theology, is representative of real men. In Goethe's *Faust*, the other great account of the anima, the Mater Gloriosa who redeems Old Greybeard at the end of the work is related to humble Gretchen of Part I. And it is no fluke that principal among the harbingers of redemption are the Woman of Samaria and the woman who was a sinner from Luke 7. Goethe's summing up in the majestic final chorus is nothing less than a biography of the anima:

Alles Vergängliche	All things transitory
Ist nur ein Gleichnis;	Are as symbols sent;
Das Unzulängliche,	Earth's insufficiency
Hier wird's Ereignis;	Here finds fulfilment;
Das Unbeschreibliche,	Here the ineffable
Hier ist's getan;	Wins life through love
Das Ewig-Weibliche	The Endless Woman-soul
Zieht uns hinan.	Leads us above.

Faust is finally redeemed by the woman he first rejected. That is, we achieve integration, fulfilment, balance, completeness by means of the full and appropriate development of the anima, the woman within. She is virtuous and holy, like Mary, at the last; but she is still das Ewig-Weibliche and what is lowly. What is redeemed is never wiped out; nor is any aspect of what does the redeeming. So the temptress and the sinner, the companion and the mother, are all present in the redeeming woman who appears in that rocky place with Dr Marianus at the conclusion of Goethe's greatest work. In psychological terms we really are saved by our weaknesses as well as by our strengths. In fact that is the only way of salvation which avoids hubris.

I have concentrated attention on the form in which this story of redemption (of the integration of man's personality) finds

expression in the life of Jesus as set down in the New Testament.
But this is not the only place where the same story is to be found.
I mentioned *Faust* but I might also have referred to the whole
mythology of Western civilization, to fairy tales and even
(especially) to the mythologizing tendencies of popular television
series. None of these sources should be regarded as irrelevant
since they are all the imaginative creations of the mind of man
which throughout the centuries has exhibited a consistency, a
sameness, a similarity in the way it has developed. We expect
creations to reveal the personality of the creator and that is exactly
what our invented myths and fictions do. All these things are *untrue*
only in the most trivial sense. In the deepest psychological and
spiritual sense they are inescapably *true*. Anyone who denies these
truths soon finds himself in the business of inventing a rival system
or mythology which turns out in the end to be only the original
system in a different guise. A long time ago Bertrand Russell
showed how this is true in the comparison of those two apparently
opposed systems, Biblical Theology and Communism:

Yahweh = Dialectical Materialism
The Messiah = Marx
The Elect = The Proletariat
The Church = The Communist Party
The Second Coming = The Revolution
Hell = The Punishment of the Capitalists
The Millennium = The Communist Commonwealth

There are many such comparisons possible. For instance there
is the correspondence between Christian doctrine and the concepts
of Jungian psychology where the functions of Christ and the Ego,
the Devil, and the Shadow, Eve/Mary and the Anima, God and
the Self are psychologically interchangeable. It soon becomes clear
that in all these things we are dealing with a recurring pattern of
expression which lies deep within the human personality. *Perhaps
we are dealing with the structure of personality itself.* No wonder that the
themes and characters repeat themselves. This does not relativize
them or in any way make them less true; on the contrary it
reinforces the view that psychological and spiritual truth is a unity.
In the same way, the New Testament does not become a lesser
revelation because it is susceptible to comparison with other
literature in which the same themes and patterns present them-

selves. In fact, the way in which 'sacred' and 'profane', 'serious' and 'popular' literature corroborate one another ought to be a reassurance to modern man who in his anxiety begins to harbour doubts about the ancient truths. The capacity to see these basic similarities in the literature of Western civilization has been greatly increased by new discoveries and techniques in literary criticism under the name of Structuralism. However, theories about spiritual and psychological truths are of more interest to some people than to others; what can not be evaded is the existence of spiritual and psychological realities. These remain part of our experience no matter which religious or secular language we use to refer to them.

The anima is one of the most powerful of these realities; more powerful still because it is an unconscious aspect – the woman within corresponding to the mysterious woman of literature who can be both virgin and *femme fatale*. In practical terms the qualities belonging to the anima are easily describable and they take contrasting forms. The dark side of the anima, the *femme fatale*, the siren and so on corresponds to all the unworthy and only half-articulated ideas, desires and fantasies which are to be found in man's unconscious: the chaos and turmoil of the unconscious mind which erupts into consciousness in bizarre and numinous dreams and which sometimes plagues our waking existence with chaotic fantasies and passions. A man in the grip of the anima is often conspicuous for his wild and irrational behaviour. It is a similar experience to being enchanted or being in love, though it was Freud and not Jung who said that that sort of love is a universal neurosis.

With his conscious mind man likes to think that he is in control of himself, the master of his own house. But this is only part of the truth. In reality the personality of man is much larger than consciousness alone; it consists of the whole world of the unconscious as well. Psychological progress, spiritual development and self-knowledge occur when consciousness and unconsciousness are in proper balance and the conscious man is being enriched and enlarged by the dialogue with his unconscious. In the old religious language this stands for the same experience as prayer and a right relationship with God, doing his will and so on. Just as our religious tradition has always maintained that God's resources are infinite, that he is always sufficient for us and more than we can either desire or deserve, so the resources of the unconscious are without limit. There is always space in which the personality can grow. But this growth is a subtle and delicate business and we must learn to read what often look like coded signs if we are to make progress.

The chaotic visions and passions aroused by the anima must not be denied or projected but used in the same way that the Shadow must be used. Man who prides himself on his analytical intellect and rationality must learn to accept that there is another side to his nature, one involving emotion, irrationality and the intuitive faculty. Examples from history show all too plainly what tragedy occurs when this side is denied. For instance, in olden times man afflicted by his own psychic imbalance and emotional chaos, projected this on to the 'objective' woman. So they burned witches – burned them for producing an enchantment that was actually the work of man's own unconscious. In more recent times the suppression of the anima has again resulted in projection as man has rejected women's equal rights. Something akin to these social phenomena occurs also on the individual, personal level. The man who denies his anima restricts and finally halts the growth of his personality. Typically he is strict, with himself as well as with others, overcontrolled, serious, lacking the perspective of humour. Frequently he inhabits a resentful marriage and disapproves of his young daughters. But the anima which he suppresses can never be completely denied, so perhaps it explodes into consciousness from time to time in neurotic outbursts of temper or in periodical indiscipline and binges. Such a man is in an uncomfortable predicament, but his case is by no means hopeless. A suppressed anima will always give plenty of hints that it is still alive. He must learn to interpret these hints which may come through his dreams or waking fantasies. He can help himself by what might seem irrelevant practical measures: taking more interest in his wife and in her activities or starting a hobby which occupies that side of his personality which is not involved in his work and routine. Family doctors have long known the psychotherapeutic value of hobbies for those among their patients who suffer 'with their nerves'.

The anima is particularly dangerous in mid-life and even later than that. Jung says, 'When a respectable septuagenarian runs off with a red-haired chorus girl of twenty-two we know that the gods have claimed another victim'. The forty year old man who has worked conscientiously for twenty years and provided for his wife and children may suddenly 'catch sight of' the unconscious side of his personality and project this on a young woman. This is a frequent cause of marital breakdown because the man really believes he has found in the young girl something of inestimable value that he has been missing all these years. Indeed he has been missing something, but this is the woman within who has attached herself to the sweetheart. Because these experiences spring from the depths of the unconscious they are charged with a numinous power and they become irresistible. No wonder the poor lovestruck middle-aged man refers to the young woman as 'the girl of my dreams'; that is exactly what she is – though in a sense which he does not understand.

But, while the dangerous characteristics of the anima need to be mentioned, it is important not to neglect the positive side. We have already seen how the search for wisdom (sophia) can be a means of establishing a proper relationship with the unconscious forces; the stories of Eve and Mary, Gretchen and the Ewig-Weibliche, the women present at the empty tomb speak of the healing and redemptive power of the anima. In psychological terms this means that a proper balance of consciousness and the unconscious leads to a development and flowering of the personality which is otherwise impossible. The unconscious forces will work on our behalf but, because they are unconscious, there is always the dark and bewildering aspect involved. One of the most prominent images of the unconscious is the forest in fairy tales. Another is the sea, even the Sea of Galilee upon which Christ conducted much of his ministry. We should not forget his words 'Launch out into the deep' (Luke 5.4).

We have lived for thousands of years in a culture dominated by males and the masculine aspect, and so most of our art and literature has been produced by men. Naturally this literature will deal with psychological and spiritual matters mainly from the man's point of view. It needs to be said therefore that all these words about the eternal feminine and the reality of the anima are only one side of the story: women have in their unconscious the male archetype, the animus, and this bears just the same relationship to her consciousness and plays the same part in her development as the anima plays in the case of men. The animus exists in myth as, for instance, the prince who cuts his way through the forest (of unconsciousness) in order to be united with the maiden who is imprisoned in the middle of it. He exists also in his dark aspect as the seducer and the rake, as the numinously dissolute Heathcliffe of *Wuthering Heights*, as the incubus. But he is also present in the heavenly child and in the hero. The psychology of women thus differs in particular from that of men but, in all major respects relating to structure and dynamics, the psychological processes are alike. Man is consciously male and unconsciously female while in the woman the structure is reversed. In both cases there needs to be a proper balance of consciousness with the unconscious forces (anima or animus) if there is to be a full development of the personality.

4 | The Father is greater than I

The person referred to by Jesus as his Father is with him throughout the years of his ministry; indeed we have seen that the Father was present from much earlier, from the time of Jesus' visit to the temple when he was twelve years old. And the voice of the Father speaks at his baptism in the Jordan. The gospels lead us to understand that Jesus derives his strength and his purpose from the Father. Time and again he retires to the desert or to a quiet, solitary place to pray. What is the Father like?

He is the God of the Old Testament having undergone a transformation from the bellicose and capricious spirit who rumbles in the wilderness like a storm cloud, who calls down fire on Sodom or who commands that Israel's enemies should be utterly destroyed (I Sam. 15.33) to one with whom it is possible to have an intimate relationship. Jews of the Old Testament period were, it is true, taught by the Psalmists to think of God as the Shepherd of Israel and in that compassionate prophetic book Hosea, he is likened to a loving and forgiving husband, but it was Jesus himself who spoke of God as Abba – the familiar Aramaic word for Father which Jeremias has translated as Daddy (Mark 14.36).

Most of the New Testament sayings about the Father appear in St John's Gospel and they represent the theologizing work of the writer rather than the actual words of Jesus. But this should cause no dismay. For good or ill, all our images of Jesus come to us through the writings of other people and it is only to be expected that these men should have their own points of view. So the theological perspective of Luke is different from that of Mark, and John is different from them both. However, there are points of consensus and common themes, and the relationship of Jesus with his Father – though made more of in John's Gospel than in the others – is an issue which features in all the gospels.

In that philosophical prologue with which he begins his gospel, John says that Jesus has a unique relationship with the Father; he is 'as the only begotten' (John 1.14). Again, 'The Father loveth the Son, and hath given all things into his hand' (John 3.35). Sometimes there seems to be a dichotomy about this relationship and we must contrast passages such as –

> The Son can do nothing of himself, but what he seeth the Father do (John 5.19).
> And I will pray the Father . . . (John 12.27).

with other verses like –

> The Father is in me, and I in him (John 10.38).
> He that hath seen me hath seen the Father (John 14.9).
> I and my Father are one (John 10.30).

The first set of texts suggest a certain dependence or even subordinate status, while the second set indicate equality and a relationship of identity. This is a problem which was not solved until the invention of the doctrines of the Trinity; and some would argue that it was not adequately solved even then. As in the earlier studies of the Shadow and the anima, once again analytical psychology can help provide an explanation which is not merely abstract and theoretical but one which we discover to be true within our experience. This is the doctrine of the Self.

In his study of human personality, Jung said that consciousness is not the only aspect; there is also the unconscious represented primarily to consciousness by the anima. But he further claimed that consciousness and the unconscious together form a whole. This whole, containing ego and shadow and other archetypal characters besides the anima, he called the Self. This Self is the completing, individualing principle of personality. We may picture it as both origin and goal of our being. It is what we are, our-Self, and yet, because it is both conscious and unconscious, it is transcendent over the conscious ego – that part of us that we frequently and misleadingly refer to as ourself. In other words the archetype of the Self is much like the person of the Father in St John's Gospel.

Jesus, says John, came to do the will of the Father (John 4.34) and to reveal his glory (John 14.13). And because Jesus showed obedience to his Father and followed his vocation perfectly, the Father was perfectly revealed in him so that 'He that hath seen me hath seen the Father' (John 14.19). But it is also in the purposes and plan of the Father that his Son should die and then be raised up that all men see his glory and share his life (John 17.1–2). This glory and this life are of God the Father himself (John 17.5).

This pattern of life, of obedience and sacrifice, is described in the Gospels as doing the will of God; and, as it says in the Epistle to the Hebrews, the person Jesus who did these things is 'the brightness of his glory, and the express image of his person' (Heb. 1.3) and as John says 'the Word (who) was God' (John 1.1). The purpose of Jesus' life then was to reveal God. And, as Jesus said, the purpose of his followers' lives is to do the same (John 20.21). They do this by being like Jesus; that is the meaning of John 14.6 'I am the way, the truth, and the life: no man cometh unto the Father but by me'. It is the meaning of the phrase which ends so many prayers and thanksgivings, 'through Jesus Christ our Lord'. It is in this sense that Jesus is the pattern of life for all men. God is revealed in him and in all men who follow his way, who learn and appropriate to themselves the truth that was his life. Believing in Jesus (John 3.16) and trusting in him means that we perceive his life as the eternal model of godliness and man's true destiny. It is not a case of believing that certain facts about Jesus will somehow save us at the judgment; but that the only way to the abundant quality of life which the New Testament calls 'eternal life' is by going the same way as Jesus. Once again the outward events of the story of Jesus have inward, psychological and spiritual significance for us. We may not work miracles, be crucified and rise again from the dead, but these events are pictures of the inner truth about the life of everyman. The effects in us are the same whether we use the old biblical language or any other, but perhaps the terminology of analytical psychology is more helpful in an age which can make little sense of the strident supernaturalism of the first-century documents. But this is just one more way of telling the same story.

The story begins with man as ego, his waking consciousness. First he must learn to come to terms with the dark side of that ego, the Shadow. Only then can he begin to respond to the signals and messages which arise out of the unconscious and whose goal is the individuation or making whole (salvation) of the total personality, consciousness and unconscious together. Our earliest false impression is that the ego is the whole personality, so when we encounter the Shadow we are brought up with a jolt. Something similar happens when we come into contact with the anima. But even Shadow and anima are only incomplete aspects of the whole. The issue is one of accommodation and balance. In biblical terminology that word 'accommodation' means 'sacrifice'.

In the child, who does not at first differentiate between himself and his environment, there exists a rudimentary wholeness. The beginnings of language – 'In the beginning was the Word' (John 1.1) – and growth gradually produce the differentiated ego. This is a kind of kenosis or self-emptying and it is paralleled in Christian theology by the divine emptying himself in order to redeem all things (Phil. 2.5–11). If the son had not been born as a man for us we could not know the way of salvation; if the ego does not emerge separately from the undifferentiated immaturity of infancy, there can be no process of individuation. These two statements mean the same thing. When the trials and integrations (temptations) concerning the Shadow and the anima have been met – though these are, being eternally present, never over and done with – symbols of totality begin to make their appearance. This is the increasing perception of God's presence; alternatively it can be described as the emergence of the archetype of the Self. Traditional images of God are much like personifications of the archetype of the Self: the Wise Old Man, Sarastro in *Die Zauberflöte* for instance, or even the Old Man with a beard of popular mythology.

An awareness of the presence of God or of the need for God emerges at different times in the lives of different people. A literary sign of its appearance in the story of Jesus is of course the voice at his baptism. Although it is true that many people have an awareness of God from very early in their lives, it is also true that in most people's experience there is a sharpening of this awareness towards the second part of life. Jung speaks of the first phase of life, up to about forty as a journey outwards and the second phase as the journey inwards. The biblical metaphor of heaven or death as

'home' finds echoes here (Eccles. 12.5). At any rate the issue of
God often returns with added poignancy as a man ages. Or,
in psychological jargon, the middle-aged man begins the more
earnestly to crave wholeness of being. This wholeness is purchased
at cost to the insistent ego which must learn to be quiet and listen
to the voice of the Self. In the biblical language, to become
subordinate to the will of God. In one sense it is a transition from
the active to the passive voice. I know a composer, Edward Cowie,
whose creative work followed exactly this pattern. For years he
was a highly intellectual serial composer preoccupied with his
standing among the avant garde. When he was about thirty-five
he broke loose from merely theoretical restraints and, as he put it,
began to *listen* to the music he was producing.

In the religious language we say that we cannot be saved unless
we give our lives to God as revealed perfectly in Christ; in the
language of psychology we say that we cannot achieve wholeness
of being (individuation) unless the ego sees itself as but one aspect
of the total Self. The first part of life is rightly a time of doing and
achieving of outwardness – the conquering hero's adventures as a
young man. But it is inappropriate for the 'Mature' man to behave
as if he were still a youth, and when we see this happening perhaps
we smile. The man in the parable frenetically building more barns
was surely of this sort; but God pointed out his mistake:

> Thou fool, this night thy soul shall be required of thee: then
> whose shall those things be, which thou hast provided? (Luke
> 12.20)

The man had rejected the development of his soul and his spiritual
poverty was therefore starkly revealed to him before the imminence
of death. He should have given the farm to his son and sat himself
down by the fireside to ponder or only to dream. I am not
recommending quietism by saying that there is a different style of
living, an orientation of the soul, appropriate to the second part of
life from that which was proper in the first part. Though it sounds
stark, there is truth in the saying that youth is a preparation for
life and maturity is a preparation for death.

During the first part of life a man builds up resources of
experience through all the usual events which happen – his
choosing a career, marrying, raising children and so on. It is this
fund of experience which is the raw material for the full flowering

of his personality and the job of the second half of life is to order inwardly all this raw material in a way which is unique for every person. 'Crabbed age and youth' says Shakespeare, but age need not be crabbed. If the middle-aged man will begin to attend to his inwardness – if he will, as it were, stop chasing about building more barns and start instead to look at what he has in his barns already – he will have a good chance of avoiding the frustration and despair which comes with old age. When a man gets past middle life he needs some inwardness on which to live or else he will only feel disappointed and afraid: disappointed because he has not achieved as much as he hoped he might have done; afraid as he daily senses the weakening of his natural powers and the onset of ailments which the doctor annoyingly puts down to 'old age'. And if he has had children, this is the time when they will be leaving home to start families of their own. Though a man may have looked forward to the marriages of his children as events after which he might enjoy 'a bit of peace and quiet', the reality is often quite different. Suddenly the noise and rush has gone, together with all the demands that used to be made on his time. He did not realize before how much his life was involved with his growing children. He begins to feel that he is no longer of any use. This is also a time when many marriages come under strain; man and wife alone in the house realize how much or how little they have in common. At a time when he feels emotionally-drained by events, he finds that he is having to put some hard work into his marriage. The same is true for the woman of course who also has to suffer the sundry pains and disillusionments of the menopause.

In all these things it is the soul that we ourselves have been creating and furnishing during the first part of our lives which must now sustain us. It is no use projecting our discontent on to the world and blaming external events and people for our unhappiness – that old Shadow again. We must learn to live on what we have gathered: 'There is nothing from without a man, that entering into him can defile him: but the things which come out of him, those are they that defile the man' (Mark 7.15).

I do not mean to suggest that the second part of life must turn out to be a disappointment, a fretful dwindling, full of bitterness and regret; but too often it does turn out this way. You can tell a lot from the anxiety in people's faces, in their expressions and postures. As the poet C. H. Sisson says, 'The body is a record of the mind'. Some old faces, on the contrary, look transcendent, victorious; scarred by experience perhaps but finally triumphant. I have five photographs of the composer Gustav Mahler all taken at different times; in sequence these demonstrate the maturity that can be attained. (They are reproduced in Henry Raynor's book *Mahler*). Far from being a disappointment and an anticlimax, the second part of life can be a period of fulfilment greater than anything belonging to the early years. It should be the time when a man knows himself and feels at home with himself, when he is not constantly displeased looking at himself in the mirror, counting the grey hairs and the wrinkles and hoping to catch sight of a younger image of himself. 'I have learned, in whatsoever state I am, therewith to be content' (Phil. 4.11).

There is a paradox in the discovery of the Self for while it is certainly a gradual revelation of fullness (the *pleroma* of Ephesians 4.13), it is also a process of letting go, of readiness for death. It is simultaneously an experience of one's identity and a willingness to let go of that identity, something akin to disinterestedness – the perspective of eternity as the body of time. Or, as Aristotle says, 'Call not a man happy until he is dead'. Examples from the world of art and music abound. Mahler again: in his early days he composed vast symphonies possessed by the romantics of atonement. He wrote, 'Why do we live? Why do we suffer? Why do we die? Is all this just a horrible jest? We must answer these questions if we are to go on living; if we are only to go on dying.' As if these questions could ever be answered! But in his later years, Mahler learned an acceptance and a serenity which is perfectly expressed in *Abschied* from *Das Lied Von Der Erde* and in the last movement of the *Ninth Symphony*. The music corresponds to the photographs.

The mystical theologians, speaking an older religious language, knew also about the void and the spiritual paradox whereby we know God through his *absence* as well as through his presence. Death itself should hold no terrors for the Christian because what he calls God is greater than death. In the language of analytical psychology this translates into the realization that the experience of completeness designated by the word 'Self' gives a new and calm prospect to the fact of one's own mortality. The man who is discovering his true Self ('being saved' in the older language) knows that by the side of this experience death is unimportant.

'O death, where is thy sting? O grave, where is thy victory?'
(I Cor. 15.55) says St Paul. And he says in the next verses,

> The sting of death is sin, and the strength of sin is the law. But
> thanks be to God, which giveth us the victory through Our Lord
> Jesus Christ (I Cor. 15.56–57).

And what is sin, what was it ever except falling short (Greek
hamartia)? This is old metaphor taken from the archery contests
and *hamartia* is the falling short of the arrows in front of the target.
And in psychological terms the same is true; sin is that state in
which we find ourselves when we fall short of the individuation of
the true Self. 'For what is a man profited, if he shall gain the whole
world and lose his own soul?'

If the Self is the integrating factor in our development, if it exists
and operates solely for the good of our whole being, then why do
we resist its promptings? Why do we not welcome gladly the signs
of its presence? The answer is that our ego, our conscious mind,
does not really believe that integration with the Self is a good thing.
This is because whenever the Self appears it demands radical
changes in the way we order our lives. In religious terms this is
nothing other than the call to repentance and conversion which
men have always resisted, thinking that salvation is either irrelevant or available by some less uncomfortable path. 'It is a fearful
thing to fall into the hands of the living God' (Heb. 10.31). As God
is greater than man, so the archetype of the Self is transcendent
over the desires and affections of the ego. And the ego must be
prepared to lose itself in the encounter with all the fullness of the
Self: 'Thou fool, that which thou sowest is not quickened except it
die' (I Cor. 15.37).

In the story of the life of Jesus this saying about death is given
literal expression; and his death must occur before the resurrection
and the life everlasting. Jesus does not face his death without fear.
In the Garden of Gethsemane the Father who has inspired his
ministry becomes the Almighty who inspires terror according to
St Mark:

> Abba, Father, all things are possible unto thee; take away this
> cup from one . . . (Mark 14.34).

St Matthew says the same. St Luke records his very human
anguish:

And being in an agony he prayed more earnestly: and his sweat
was as it were great drops of blood falling down to the ground
(Luke 22.44).

Only John, for whom the story of Christ is far more stylized and
theologized, has him ready to face his death without qualms:

And now, O Father, glorify thou me with thine own self with
the glory which I had with thee before the world was (John
17.5).

These are not the original words of Jesus but words put into his
mouth by a sophisticated theologian well-acquainted with the
Greek philosophers and with the idea of the pre-existent Word
(Logos) who is the organizing and spiritualizing divine principle
at work in the world. But we do not have to choose between the
more realistic record of the other three gospel writers and the
stylized approach of John; all the sources reveal something of the
truth about Jesus' prayer before his arrest, and consequently the
truth for us about how we should prepare for our own physical
death and for the encounter with the Self which is a death of
another kind.

The synoptic writers tell us that Jesus was afraid. They are
writing as if they were there at the event. We are meant to know
that, in the turmoil and uncertainty of Gethsemane, Jesus was
genuinely afraid. This is a way of reaffirming his human nature.
Any man would have been afraid. If we had John's account alone,
we should surely feel as if something was missing. Does a man
really go to an agonizing death his mouth full of sophisticated
explications about his destiny and his intimacy with the divine?
Men as we know men certainly do not. The synoptics are reassuring
because they tell us that *even* Jesus was afraid at that moment. John
is reassuring in a different way because all that theologizing of the
issue shows that there is a purpose and a plan and that the end of
that plan is glorious. Mark writes as if he does not know what is
going to happen next. John writes as if from the standpoint of
eternity.

In the synoptic gospels, and particularly in St Mark, we are
offered a realistic account of a death by crucifixion; in St John we
are offered a description of that death but also a theological
evaluation of its purpose and significance. Mark has only one word

spoken by Jesus from the cross – the cry of dereliction: 'My God, my God, why hast thou forsaken me?' (Mark 15.35). It is possible that Jesus uttered this terrible cry, but it is perhaps more likely that Mark is putting the opening words of Psalm 22 to a new theological use. In that psalm we have the lament of the King who was symbolically killed in the fertility ritual of the syncretistic cult practised in ancient Israel. Mark clearly intends to tell his readers that Jesus too is a king and that his death is part of a plan which issues in new life. But he puts no triumphant verses into the mouth of Jesus, no words of commendation or forgiveness such as we find in the other Gospels. Whatever the final result of Jesus' death – and there are only the barest hints in Mark 16.1–8 which verses are the original ending of his gospel – it is made plain that so far as Jesus himself was concerned the event was one of terror and loss of faith. In fact the whole of Mark's Gospel is the story of the progressive alienation of Jesus. First he is deserted by the crowds who once followed him enthusiastically; then his family and friends turn against him; Judas betrays him; at Gethsemane the disciples forsake him; even Peter (the visionary of Mark 8.27ff.) denies him; finally, on Calvary, Jesus loses his trust in God in the utterance of that terrible cry.

This is our story too for this is how we must face life and death. In the end, like Jesus, each of us is alone. All men live and all men die but no one can live my life and die my death but myself. We have supporters, comforters, family and friends – perhaps even a faith by which we are sustained, but fundamentally we are alone. If this is true of our physical life in the world, it is true also of our inner, spiritual and psychological life. Each one of us must come to terms with evil in the world and evil in himself (the Shadow); each must discover his own soul (anima); and each must face the encounter with the Self which constitutes a spiritual death and resurrection.

This spiritual process can be described in many different ways but whether we choose the language of sacrifice, of loss or of killing, the experience is the same. There comes a time in our lives when we have to let go of what we think is ourself in order to discover our true Self. This is giving up the world for God's sake; it is drinking of the cup (of his death) of which Christ drank; it is the submission of the ego to the Self. And, like the crucifixion, this must always happen in the dark (Mark 15.33) because, just as in

Mark's gospel God is absent, the fullness of the Self has not yet appeared and the only immediate experience is of spiritual death. We must lose our life before we can find it (Matt 10.39). Only when there are no props left, no comfort, so friendly encouragement, no faith, do we face the truth which in the new mythology of analytical psychology is described as the Self. John has Jesus say he is one with his Father (John 10.30) but, paradoxically, he also says 'My Father is greater than I' (John 14.28). The ancient and mysterious doctrine of the Trinity explained paradoxes such as these by saying that Jesus and his Father were two Persons in the Substance of the Triune Godhead. The new and perhaps equally mysterious symbolism of analytical psychology attempts to explain the inner experience to which this ancient doctrine corresponds by saying that the ego is but part of the total Self. The destiny of the Christian is to become the Child of God (Rom 8.16, 21; 9.8) and indeed he is already that in a rudimentary sense; but his complete sanctification must wait for the end of all things. Similarly, the ego partakes of the nature of the Self, but it is only an imperfect copy, a part of the Self; the full emergence of the Self comes only after a lifetime of spiritual and psychological experience. In the old religious language, God is all in all at the end of time. So I may hope to know my identity (my true Self) after much inner struggle and development and towards the end of this life.

This process of sanctification (classical spirituality) or individuation (analytical psychology) is always a tremendous struggle because it seems to be leading us towards an end that is arid. We should take comfort from the fact that it was the Spirit of God which led Jesus into the wilderness. Our inclination is to pull in the opposite direction, in the direction of what St Paul calls 'the flesh' which is a term standing for ambition. Ambition is, of course, the identifying mark of the ego, but it is only when we cease to rely on the strivings of the ego that we discover the true Self. A hard lesson, especially since so much of the advice we receive in the early part of life is to build up the forces of the ego, to work and to strive. This advice is necessary and good, but we should not mistake the task of the ego for the task of the whole Self. But neither should we denigrate or suppress the ego prematurely. It must first be allowed to have full development before it takes its place in the larger Self. The image is one of fruition (Mark 4.20) not of suicide. This needs to be stressed in our own time when many quasi-religious cults are offering something that amounts to ego-extinction to would-be adherents. There is a fashion for 'getting rid of negative mind' and 'escaping from the tyranny of the ego'. In fact, nothing could be more unhelpful. The goal of spiritual unity consists in a proper balance between conscious and unconscious forces, between thinking aspects and feeling aspects, between rationality and what is irrational. It is just as great a mistake to deny the place of rational thinking, of the conscious ego, as it is to reject the unconscious factors the anima and the Self. The man who is overcontrolled and who tries to live exclusively within the calculating ego will never achieve a whole, balanced personality. But the man who, seeing that rationality has its limits, decides to abandon it as useless is making an equal and opposite error. The rationalizing, categorizing ego is always necessary first as that which receives the numinous and puzzling messages which arise from the unconscious mind and secondly to put these in some sort of order. The alternative is to be overwhelmed by unconscious contents and to lose a proper sense of personal identity. Some of the irrationalist cults have thought far enough to realize this consequence, but realization has generally led to their making a virtue out of ego loss and to the claim that individual identity is a spiritual and psychological handicap – something to be got rid of. But the actual result of ego-loss is a hopelessly one-sided emphasis and attitude which in some cases amounts to psychosis and other severe disorders of the personality. Indeed, what else should we expect to occur once half the personality is denied and disowned in this way?

The doctrine of the resurrection of the dead is a powerful symbolic warning: man does not vanish into impersonality but his complete self including the ego is preserved and transformed. That is one of the reasons behind the insistence in all the resurrection appearance that Jesus was no phantom, no mere emanation from some impersonal realm, but that he was who he had always been. He was recognizably Jesus. The principle of identity and distinctiveness is of course the ego. The desire for individuality and for its continuation as consciousness is to be seen in the ordinary hope among men and women of many religions and none that in the afterlife we shall recognize our friends and be recognized by them.

In the Synoptic Gospels the crucifixion is not the conclusion of the gospel. Something is felt to be lacking and this is supplied by the stories about the resurrection. John has resurrection appearances in his gospel of course but there is a sense in which these are only postscripts; for John the climax of the gospel story occurs at the crucifixion itself. In John's account there is no cry of dereliction. How could there be such a cry from one who, according to the theologized narrative, has claimed to be at one with the Father and who has complete understanding of the purpose of his death together with foreknowledge about the Spirit-filled community that was to follow his death? John's Jesus sees his death as a glorification (John 17.5) and he is able to speak confidently to his Roman accuser about the precise relationship between the powers of this world and their limits and the power of God (John 19.10–11). And the last words of Jesus are not of despair but of triumph: 'It is finished' meaning 'it is accomplished' or 'it is completed' (John 19.30). What is it that is accomplished? In theological terms the total life of obedience to the will and purposes of the Father and the glorification of the Son. It is the Amen to those words which were spoken at the beginning of Jesus' ministry: 'Thou art my beloved Son' (Mark 1.11). In psychological language this is the achievement of individuation, the perfect balance of all the forces of the personality, conscious and unconscious.

I do not mean to deny the validity of the theological account by offering a psychological perspective but to demonstrate how the theological doctrines of sacrifice and atonement are experienced within the individual. This experience is a psychological reality which finds literary and theological expression in the story of Jesus. That is why the story of Jesus remains fascinating. His story is our story too. His story is written on the historical-mythological level; ours is told on the psychological-spiritual plane. The story remains the same and there can be no question of extolling the truth or the importance of either version at the expense of the other. Unless everything that happened to Jesus could be psychologically and spiritually correlated with our experience, then the story would, quite literally and as a matter of definition, be meaningless. We should never see any significance in it. We *do* see the story of Jesus as significant precisely because we recognize it as our own on the psychological level where it is indubitable because it is part of us, the way we are.

To summarize. I have tried to show how the events in the life of

Jesus correspond with our internal process of psychological and spiritual development. Nothing can be excluded: dark and unpleasant aspects must be integrated within the whole; this is illustrated by the Gospel accounts of Jesus' conversations with the Devil and, within ourselves, by the need to develop a realistic perception of the Shadow. The dimension of psychological opposition must be acknowledged. This means that we must reconcile opposites within our own personality. The thinking aspect must accommodate the feeling aspect; what is intellectual must also take account of what is intuitive. This was described in relation to the unconscious forces of the anima which go through many stages just as artistic representations of the same archetype go through different manifestations from *Ewig-Weibliche* to Redeemer, from Eve to Mary. Finally, our experience shows that the strongest force in the personality is that which Jung calls the Self. The Self stands in relation to the rest of the psyche in much the same way as God stands in relation to the world. It is a transcendent function but one which is also part of the whole personality – as God is said by the classical theologians to be present in the world, to be immanent. In saying that the ego has a sacrificial relationship with the Self, I cautioned against the view that the aim of the individuation process (the process of salvation and of sanctification) is ego-extinction. It is not. Rather it is the development of a balanced relationship between ego and Self. In all this discussion I mean to emphasize that a psychological account such as I have given is never meant to denigrate or detract from traditional ways of talking about God and the spiritual life. But for an increasing number of people the classical supernatural account – which may be valid in itself – does not provide the intellectual and emotional satisfaction which comes from a delineation of psychological contents. It is not a case of one account being false and the other true. It is simply a fact of contemporary experience that the psychology of religious contents seems more direct, more immediate and more helpful than the old supernaturalist scheme. There is nothing particularly new in this. It is only another way of saying what Coleridge said more than a century ago: 'I am weary of proofs of religion. Make a man feel its truth for himself.'

III PRAYER

1 | Introduction

Prayer is not a form of words. It is not even an activity. It is a disposition or an attitude. The man of prayer is the one who puts himself quite self-consciously into a particular relationship with God and who then remains in that relationship twenty-four hours a day. This relationship is one that provides the man with a God's eye view of himself. It is the beginning and the end of spiritual growth. In psychological terms, prayer is the practical result of acknowledging the transcendent power of the Self over the ego. It is the conscious mind's willingness to attend to the forces of the unconscious. Atheism is never theoretical, but practical. In traditional terms the atheist is the man who believes himself to be his own origin; he does not think that he needs the sustaining power of God's presence. The modern equivalent of this practical atheism is to be found in the attitude of the man who does not appreciate the power of the Self; he lives as if ego were all. Just as the old unbelief was said to lead to damnation, so the new unbelief results in disorientation and incompleteness as the conscious and unconscious aspects of the personality cannot be brought together while ever some of those aspects are denied. In the old language, man becomes whole and holy by walking with God; in psychological terms, he achieves a measure of integration by the ego's dialogue with the unconscious. But while words are often a part of the relationship of prayer, they are not its basis. At our Confirmation classes we were taught that there are four sorts of prayers – adoration, confession, thanksgiving and supplication. I would like

to look briefly again at these categories both from the position of
the old tradition and that of the analytical psychologist.

2 | Adoration

Verbal expression of the act of adoration is traditionally given in the words of, for instance, the *Sanctus* – 'Holy, Holy, Holy, Lord God of Hosts. Heaven and earth are full of thy glory; glory be to thee O Lord most high' – or in the opening words of the *Te Deum* or other hymn of praise. These are the propositions of ecstasy. They are, however, not true propositions; they do not describe, for that to which they are addressed is beyond description. God is always beyond description. That is the meaning of his transcendence. To imagine that one can describe God is to come perilously close to idolatry. Because God is beyond the limits of language, both the positive and negative ways of adoration are possible for man. Positive adoration uses poetry, music, psalms and hymns in order to express something of the rapture of this kind of prayer; but it still recognizes that these expressions in no way confine or restrict God in the way that a definition confines and restricts. Negative aspects of adoration are linked with passivity and a refusal to attempt expression of any kind. They include the physical and mental stillness of 'Be still then and know that I am God' (Ps. 46.10). There is no reason why either sort of prayer should be extolled to the other's detriment – though there is a strong mystical affirmation of the passive, quiet way of contemplation. This sort of prayer is the opposite of all forms of verbalization and of all image-making. Indeed it is the quieting of the imagination. It is *being* rather than *doing*. But it takes as much (if not more) effort as active adoration because the mind's interior monologue, the chattering stream of consciousness, will not easily be silenced. Active adoration concentrates attention on the being of God and makes sounds and poems about him – poems and sounds which, nonetheless, it recognizes as inadequate to the subject to which they are addressed. It is as if the soul erupts into sound because it cannot help itself. The passivity of contemplation, imageless as it is, focusses upon nothing; but the contemplative mystic knows that God is to be affirmed even in his absence.

This profound affirmation accords with the immediacy and undeniability of our inner experience and it makes a nonsense of purely intellectual and discursive arguments about the nature of God. It transcends the traditional Atheistic-Theistic divide as can be seen by a comparison of two writers who used and commended forms of contemplation. The first, Père de Caussade, stands in the classic tradition of Western spirituality. We are to abandon ourselves utterly to divine providence and to live in the sacrament of the moment. This is the spiritual interpretation of Christ's words about the lilies of the field: to give up all anxiety, to relinquish it, to allow God's reality to be sufficient for us. It does not matter, says de Caussade, what we are doing; whether we are praying, working or resting we should simply accept that the whole sub-stance and meaning of the present moment is given by God alone. The atheistic existentialist, Albert Camus, commends something in which the psychological consequences are exactly the same: to give up hope. At first glance this does not seem to be a very encouraging direction – least of all for people who have been taught to regard hope as a virtue, 'hope seen is not hope' (Rom. 8.24). But what Camus means by giving up hope is giving up the neurotic habit of living in some other time than the present, This is life and reality, literally in the *here* and *now*. We must live in *this*, not in some other time or place – neither in nostalgia nor in neurotic anticipation – but in the present. From the point of view of our experience, de Caussade and Camus are saying exactly the same thing; de Caussade uses the old God-language while Camus does not. That is to say, the difference between them is conceptual and linguistic, a matter of choosing a particular form of expression. The experienced reality, the psychological content, is the same in either case. But then the mystical theologian has always known that genuine prayer is not about words at all – not even words about God. Once again the atheistic – theistic divide is seen as trivial.

In the language of analytical psychology, active adoration consists in experience of unconscious contents as they appear to consciousness in all their many guises and disguises. The theophanous atmosphere of dreams is a particular instance; so are the assistance and corroboration given to spiritual appetites by works of art and music. In both cases the ego is brought into powerful contact with the world of other Selves, with what Jung calls the Collective Unconscious – that great reservoir of experiences and images which makes the worlds of art and dreams possible. When we feel awe or delight at the sight of a Van Gogh or a Vermeer, this is because we are being shown aspects of a shared Self by an ego who has seen the world from a different perspective. The sense of awe or other deep sense arises because what the work of art shows us behind and through its outward appearance is some previously undiscovered aspect of our own Self. This is why the arts of man are truly creative and sustaining – because they plumb the depths of a shared and only partly conscious reality for which Jung's term Collective Unconscious seems a useful label. And it does not matter whether we call what is apprehended 'God' or 'the Unconscious'; the psychological experience is the same in each case. There is no reason to idolize any particular language of evocation whether that language belongs to Aquinas or to Jung. Again the immediate concern must be beyond words and rest with that which is indubitable – the experience itself. This is the experience articulated by the Psalmist when he writes 'O Lord, thou hast searched me out and known me' (Ps. 139.1).

It has become something of a commonplace in religious discussion to claim that experiences of God are not always pleasant experiences. When Paul Tillich wrote a commentary on psalm 139, he said the Psalmist was not trying to express how much comforted and upheld he felt himself to be by the perpetual presence of God, but that he was disturbed and even terrified by that presence – otherwise why should he want the darkness to cover him (verse 11)? Whenever we encounter God or the archetypal images produced by the unconscious mind we are bound to be disturbed. When the prophet Isaiah had his vision of God in the temple he thought his end had come:

Holy, holy, holy is the Lord of hosts:
the whole earth is full of his glory . . .
Then said I, Woe is me! For I am undone (Isa. 6.3,5).

The writer Rudolf Otto has explained the original meaning of
the word 'holy' as something that is terrifying, untouchable in its
otherness, a threat to our spiritual equilibrium. The identification
of holiness with goodness on the other hand is a fairly recent
development. At first there was no connection between the two
concepts except through the notion of taboo. Eventually taboos
were prescribed by the written law and morality was derived from
religious experience. The Old Testament is full of man's encounter
with holiness in its original sense of awful, dreadful and terrifying.
There is Jacob's vision of which he says, 'Surely the Lord is in this
place; and I knew it not . . . How dreadful is this place! this is none
other but the house of God, and this is the gate of heaven'
(Gen. 28.16–17). Daniel speaks of the 'great and dreadful God'
(Dan. 9.4). Malachi of the 'great and dreadful day of the Lord'
(Mal. 4.5). Moses on one occasion is told that he may not see God
face to face but look only on his 'back parts' (Ex. 33.23) 'for there
shall no man see me and live (33.20). There are more than forty
descriptions in the Old Testament of God as 'terrible'. Even his
name is terrible and it acts almost like a charm so that it should
never be uttered except on rare occasions and only then by
the High Priest who has purified himself by elaborate ritual
preparations. Always there is a terrifying double aspect to God.
As Jung says, 'He *may* be loved but he *must* be feared'. The basis
of all adoration is awe.

    God is not adored for any of his qualities or aspects – *pace* the
Sabellian heresy which spoke of his aspects – but purely because
he is God. The experience of God is so overwhelming that
descriptive language is inadequate to contain it or to express it;
indeed if the experience of God's presence could be described in
this way, we should have to conclude that what was being
experienced was not God himself but some image of him. Language
about God is imagery also. When man encounters holiness it
possesses him and the reaction on his part is adoration, to be
'undone' like the prophet Isaiah. Otto's words about the moral
neutrality of these experiences is instructive here, for we speak of
a similar possession occurring when the object is thought to be

demonic. And, in the language and customs of the New Testament, we observe that spiritual forces can be cast out only by other spiritual forces. When man is possessed by the Spirit of God he often behaves as if he were mad or ecstatic. It was because of the prophetic ecstasy which he displayed that the people asked 'Is Saul also among the prophets?' (I Sam. 10.11). We think of David's dancing before the Lord (II Sam. 6.14) or again of Saul's unusual behaviour recorded in I Sam. 19.22–24. There are the four hundred ecstatic prophets of I Kings 22 and Elijah's ecstatic running before Ahab's chariot while the hand of the Lord was upon him (I Kings 18.46). In the later prophetic writings there is the vision of Ezekiel (Ezek. 1) and the vision of Isaiah in chapter 21 where, as Lindblom points out, archetypal characters emerge as an ordinary personality or functionary: 'a watchman' becomes the mysterious and numinously charged 'the watchman'. There are also many examples of the prophets, gripped by the ecstatic vision, performing symbolic actions which derive from the same psychological basis as adoration. Under the prophetic vocation an arbitrary act, one which might even appear to be a mark of insanity in another person, becomes a symbolic act charged with divine revelation: Isaiah went naked and barefoot; Jeremiah publicly smashed a bottle as a demonstration of God's imminent judgment (Jer. 19); the same prophet walked about with a yoke around his neck (chapter 27). There are many other examples of these expressions which go beyond language in their attempt to represent man's encounter with the divine.

The spiritual ecstasy which belongs to adoration is akin to madness or psychotic breakdown. It arises when a profoundly strange vision either alters the way in which reality is usually perceived or else imposes itself upon it in a manner that appears to be disordered. As objectively described, there is no difference between the seer's visions and the fantastic paintings and babblings of the lunatic. In fact, the prophet or the religious person in the ecstasy of his vision can be distinguished from the madman precisely to the extent that his irrational experience can be seen to belong to an identifiable religious tradition. Thus Ezekiel's vision is recognizable as a further revelation of the God of the Old Testament and St John's prolonged fantasy on the island of Patmos belongs to the genre of Christian apocalyptic. The point is that to the complete outsider who knows nothing of either Judaism or

Christianity, these reported experiences would appear as manifestations of psychotic dissociation. They are saved from being that by their belonging to a tradition, a system, a recognizable spiritual language.

The prophet or the religious genius always proclaims a new insight. It is as if his vision or his ecstasy occurs at the very limit of his thought and on the borderline between sanity and insanity, old revelation and new. Paul on the Damascus Road is a good example of this. He had thought out his intellectual stance against the Christian cult. He was possessed by an absolute and overwhelming desire to stamp out what he regarded as heresy. But the tensions within his own mind were overwhelming also. These broke loose and took on symbolic form in the event of his vision. From this and countless other examples, we can see that two conditions are generally necessary for genuinely prophetic utterance or for religious experience which turns out to be creative and innovatory: first the subject should have a thorough acquaintance with the tradition of which he is a representative – Paul, the priest Isaiah, Jesus himself; secondly he will be aware that what has already been spoken within the tradition is not sufficient to accommodate his present experience. Out of this crisis comes a new and disturbing religious experience which, when it has been assimilated, provides a creative development of the tradition – as for instance in the case of Jesus who translated his experience of God as Abba into a new interpretation of Judaism.

I have made these points about prophetic and religious-ecstatic experiences because, although few of us would expect to have experiences of that intensity, the spiritual and psychological life, even on the fairly mundane level follows the same pattern. That is to say, our confusion and the bankruptcy of language leads us to the silence and formlessness of adoration; and new energy, new direction in our spiritual life flows from the experience of adoration. Always there is in these events a sense both of sterility and crisis. We feel we cannot continue in what has come to seem an unsatisfactory pattern of belief, worship and even life itself. The prayer of adoration provides the creative spur. Experience is no respecter of languages. I mean to say that the subject of spiritual ecstasy and visionary experiences need not be a religious expert; sufficient that one aspect of his life seems played out, finished, and that there is an attendant emotional crisis. For instance we may cite the thousands of cases of dissociated behaviour among young people – behaviour which resembles both insanity and the strange experiences of the prophets. Not only is St Bernadette a good example here but so are all who have suffered dementia praecox or been associated with paranormal phenomena such as poltergeists at about her age. And not only these extreme examples but all whose parents have said such as 'I don't know what has come over Jane. She seems to have taken leave of her senses these days.' What has come over her and over thousands like her is the trauma of early adolescence – the end of one pattern of life and its whole repertoire of responses and the onset of a sexual crisis which is also an emotional crisis and a crisis of identity. The explicit religious connection may not be present – though in the case of Bernadette and of many others it certainly was – but the symptoms (the phenomenology) of archetypal spiritual experience are there. That is what I mean by the remark that experience is no respecter of language. These sorts of experience are very likely to attach themselves to some form of religion eventually, for the good reason that it is only the language and scheme of religious tradition which goes emotionally deep enough to provide a rational framework for such disturbances. It is no wonder that early adolescence is a peak time for religious conversions, frequently of a sudden and emotional nature, and that the same age group is encouraged to systematize its religious awareness and become more formally associated with the church – perhaps through Confirmation. The undeniable *fact* of these adolescent experiences is itself a commanding argument in favour of a strongly maintained religious tradition and for religious education. If these profound experiences are not channelled into an appropriate and well worked out system, they will produce emotional and social chaos. This realization is there even among relatively unsophisticated adults in the claim that 'there are no guidelines for the youth these days'.

But overwhelming religious experience and the sense of the holy which comes in both active and passive adoration is not confined to crucial aspects of adolescent development. To live is to change, and it is encounters with the numinous which provide the impetus for change and which help determine its direction. In psychological terms we may be said to experience what is numinous when the conscious mind is presented with one of the archetypes. No wonder then that the church has always provided ceremonies so that there may be a ritual method for the accommodation of archetypal experiences. We think of marriages, of baptisms and of funerals. Even in our so-called secular age, marriage is still popular; and even when a church marriage is not looked for, the couple frequently desire some sort of 'occasion' as a public declaration of their liaison. This is a kind of secular ritual. And if baptism no longer has its old theological connotations, it is still a valued initiation ceremony. In my parish, christenings show no sign of falling out of fashion. Scarcely anyone would think of allowing a death to pass unmarked by public ritual. Rituals are the means by which we accommodate the otherwise disordered and therefore destructive forces which assault the soul. Whether we call these forces by traditional spiritual names and locate them within a religious tradition or instead find descriptions for them in terms of the archetypes of the collective unconscious is only a matter of linguistic preference. These psychological experiences do not vanish when one becomes an intellectual athiest; they merely take on another form and turn up again under a different nomenclature. The Psalmist spoke well when he said, 'The fool hath said in his heart, There is no God' (Ps. 14.1). For it is precisely in the heart that no one can say this. I am not trying to provide an irresistible argument for the God of any particular theological definition, only to offer a demonstration of what needs no demonstrating – that common psychological experiences do not stop happening to people when when they reject 'religion' and all that it stands for.

I have taken a broad view and set a variety of experiences from the ecstasy of the prophet to the turmoil of the adolescent within the context of adoration, for this is where they belong – in that aspect of prayer which above all other aspects is concerned with what is inexpressible. I do not wish to neglect the more formalized act of adoration with which we were always taught to begin our prayers. This act is designed to give our prayers a sense of perspective, to remind us that we are men and God is God. We are finite while he is infinite. We are subject to qualification and description while he is beyond our language. Perhaps we should begin every act of adoration by reading the story of the Tower of Babel! (Gen. 11.1–9). It is because God is greater than our definitions that in adoration we do not praise him for any quality which he possesses but simply contemplate the fact of his being. This leads to an interesting conclusion which reveals a point of

contact between the spiritual traditions of the West and of the
East. We adore the living God in his being and not on account of
his qualities. In every other example we can think of, being without
qualities is a contradiction. Being stripped of all qualities would
seem to be non-being. And the Buddhists contemplate the void.
Whatever or wherever is the God whom we contemplate, the
psychological results are the same and they amount to an imaginative attempt to see ourselves from the perspective of eternity. We
are filled then with wonder, with the wonder of all the ordinary
objects round about, with unanswerable questions about our own
being and the origin and mystery of the world. Adoration raises
the level of ordinary seeing until it becomes attention. Adoration
does not allow us to take the world of experience for granted. It is
the gateway to wonder. This experience is not limited to any
particular religious language or even to the language of 'religion'
at all. Without including any reference to God or to any of the
categories of traditional spirituality, Wittgenstein expressed the
essence of adoration in the words 'It is not *how* the world is that is
mystical, but *that* it is' *(Tractatus Logico Philosophicus)*. As in the
special case of God, it is once again clear that the subject of
adoration is not any quality but being itself. Adoration is the
key to all prayer because it is the acknowledgment of what is
transcendent whether we refer to this transcendence as the being
of God or the real existence of archetypal forces beyond consciousness. The regular practice of a definite act of adoration is greatly
to be recommended as a method by which we become *deliberately*
aware of the transcendent. This has at least two functions: first it
helps guard against a sudden overwhelming outburst from the
level of unconsciousness; secondly it helps, by its very regularity,
our spiritual progress to follow an identifiable direction. Nothing
habituates like habit.

There is an ancient caution against seeking spiritual experience
for its own sake. This takes many forms and includes the prohibition
against necromancy – broken by Saul in his anxiety (I Sam. 28.11)
as well as the morbid preoccupation with spirits (I John 4.1). Paul
also, having informed his hearers of his own powerful spiritual
experiences, says that he does not glory in them (II Cor. 12.2ff.).
There is too the famous opening to the thirteenth chapter of I
Corinthians which puts all remarkable spiritual experiences within
the perspective of charity. In our own time, millions have looked

for spiritual experience – defined with scientific neutrality suitable to the secular age as 'altered states of consciousness' or (with what looks like a religious 'slip') as 'trips' ('trip' = 'pilgrimage') – through mescalin, LSD 25 and other psychedelic drugs. In every case neither the intensity nor the pleasantness/unpleasantness of the experience is of any significance. As with the prophet's vision, the test is whether an experience is true. In ordinary terms this concerns whether we are able to accommodate such spiritual experiences as we may have within the ordered course of the spiritual life. Anyone might see a vision or 'blow his mind'. The real task is to use the experience constructively and creatively within the process of psychological development. The man who takes a dose of LSD on the spur of the moment at a party is like the man who found himself casually involved with ghost hunters. And the consequences are likely to be even more shocking and unpredictable. The tale is told of the enthusiastic novice who went to his spiritual director and told him that he had had a vision of St Peter. The director smiled and sent him back to his cell. The next night he returned and reported a vision of the Blessed Virgin. The director sent him away again. The third night he came back, more enthusiastic than ever, and said, 'I know I'm making progress now father, for I have just had a vision of Our Lord himself'. The director remained calm and said simply, 'We must do something about these visions you keep having; they seem to be interfering with your prayers'. Spiritual experiences how ever weird or wonderful have no constructive effect when they are regarded merely as marvellous happenings without relation to an ordered and reflective spiritual development. In psychological terms, and to give just one example, anyone can fall under the astonishingly powerful spell of the anima – and we have seen how destructive that can be.

The act of adoration is an act of renewal for the individual because it demonstrates his will to remain open to experience. Adoration is the poetic aspect of prayer in which the one who prays sees the world and his own place in it from new perspectives. The poet's task is to make us see things in a new and perhaps even startlingly different way; the prayer of adoration is similarly creative in that it reinvests the spiritual life with new vision. It is the opposite of cliché and the antidote to prejudice. Without adoration the spiritual life would degenerate into a series of vain repetitions with no power to recreate the inner man, no material on which progress and development can build. It is the beginning of all prayer and without it genuine prayer is impossible. Where there is no adoration there is only idolatry – the constant and sterile remaking of God in worn out images.

3 | Confession

There is a basic paradox in the idea of confession: if I am really bad, sinful, depraved and so on, how can I begin to make a genuine act of contrition? Such an act would seem to require a pure and virtuous part of me, untainted by sin and therefore able to confess. But we know that the nature of sin and evil is to infect and contaminate and therefore there can be no part of our consciousness, no part of our will which is free from its taint. There are further paradoxes. For instance, if there really is a part of my will which remains free from the effects of sin and is therefore able to recognize sin and confess it, then it is precisely this part of me which has no need to confess anything. Why, or even what, should virtue confess? Too often the revivalist's injunction to confess is no more – notwithstanding all the brave talk about grace and justification by faith – than the recommendation that we pull ourselves up by our own bootstraps. This of course we cannot do. It is the will that is evil; an evil will can never confess. If the will is not evil then there is no need of confession.

The way out of this impasse can only come through the emergence of a new factor, something which gives the will a fresh insight. Spiritual writers recognize this and so they make confession follow upon adoration. In traditional language, it is the contemplation of the being of God which arouses in me a sense of my own worthlessness and sin. It is the act of adoration which gives me the sense of perspective which enables me to recognize my sinfulness and the need for contrition. Still, we may ask how this is possible since adoration itself is an act of will. The answer comes out of the understanding of adoration as something which transcends consciousness and is therefore able to influence the will. In adoration we put ourselves afresh in the presence of God who is beyond all the objects of sense and the limits of language, whose glory is 'above the heavens' (Ps. 8.1). And, as we saw in the discussion of adoration, it is the reality of what is transcendent which alone has the power to instigate change. In psychological terms it is the encounter with unconscious forces which provides the impetus for change in conscious behaviour.

Whether interpreted as a relationship between man and God or as a meeting of consciousness with the unconscious, the act of confession is an individual and personal act. This is why the intrusion of third parties has always been resented. It does not matter whether the intruder is cast in the rôle of a sacerdotal functionary with power to absolve or in the character of the tub-thumping preacher who, though he may think he has the power to convict of sin, has only the lesser power of altering the balance of sanctimoniousness. The priest cannot absolve; he can only announce the fact of absolution which is real enough as a divine gift and always available to the individual. Similarly, at the other end, as it were, of the process of penitence, the preacher can refer to sin only as a concept, as an idea – usually his own idea – and he cannot enter the relationship between the individual and God. Preachers who think they can do more about sin than this are merely Pharisees revived and proclaiming the overriding importance of what they see as 'objective truth' – in other words Law. Whereas morality, like charity, begins in the soul. The priest in the confessional may possess a card on which is written a list of sins from which the penitent may choose those he regards as most appropriate. But the penitent is not moved by these advertisements. He is moved, if at all, by the intolerable burden within his own soul. In the same way, it is no use the preacher going on about sin in terms of specific crimes – they have their favourites such as smoking, drinking and sex – which the hearer may or may not have committed. For sin is not about such crimes as belong in the legal catalogue. Sin and confession are about orientation and re-orientation, about a new way of thinking and of seeing oneself which can arise only out of that personal encounter with God, that confrontation with the forces of the unconscious. As the priest may

pronounce absolution as a fact, so the preacher may allude to
God's presence, may even evoke the presence of God in the hearts
of his hearers; but those are the limits of the priestly and evangelical
functions. When these limits are exceeded, actual damage can
occur. For instance, the 'penitent' who goes thoughtlessly to
confession and, hearing the words of confession, imagines that he
is absolved from his sins may be forestalling the true process
of penitence and reorientation. His confession of nominal sins
prevents him from seeing where his real sinfulness lies. Similarly,
the man who is made to feel uncomfortable by the preacher who
has a knack of raising topics which we all find embarrassing and
who thereupon confesses and announces his intention to give up a
few bad habits, has undergone no true rethink and reorientation
(metanoia); he has merely accepted the preacher's own prejudices
about the definition of the Christian life. Once again this is at the
cost of genuine spiritual change and progress. And it is what I
meant earlier by 'the balance of sanctimoniousness', for sometimes
it is easier to see honesty and even what is admirable in the so-
called 'sinner' than it is to see comparable qualities in the smug
band of 'the saved'.

The figure or archetype most involved in the act of confession,
the process of reorientation through rethinking, is the Devil or the
Shadow. As we noted earlier, it is foolish to imagine that this
character can be permanently cast out or otherwise eliminated,
for whenever this is alleged to have happened, he always returns
by devious or neurotic means to pervert spiritual progress once
again. For instance, anyone rejoicing at his triumph over fleshly
appetites soon begins to replace the mundane sin of gluttony with
the more dangerous sin of pride. It is worth remarking that, for
all their insistence that the 'spiritual' sins are the worst sort,
religionists never behave as if they really believed this; society,
including church and chapel society, always reserves its most prim
disgust for instances of sins of the flesh. Hence the outrage which
is frequently expressed at homosexuality or at adultery committed
by a member of the congregation. I have never heard of anyone
expelled from the Mothers' Union for backbiting or from the choir
on account of excessive pride. It is as if we do not really believe
that spiritual sins count for very much beside the more easily
identifiable sins of the flesh.

In Part II, we accepted the necessity of the Shadow, the Devil or the dark side; the part of prayer which we call confession shows clearly how that necessity functions. The Shadow calls us to constant self-examination and revaluation of our motives and attitudes without which there is no progress of any kind. As the old Catechism puts it, we are to 'renounce the Devil and all his works', but, if we are to do this, we must know what these works are. In psychological language, it is as if there is an argument between opposite poles within the psyche – an argument like that dramatic representation of Jesus with Satan in the wilderness. By forever accusing, by constantly calling our motivation into question, the Shadow provides the key to that process of self-examination which is necessary to religious development or, if you prefer one sort of jargon rather than the other, to individuation. Just as the Devil is part of the spiritual cosmos, so the shadow is part of the total Self. And the old saying about the greatest service we do the Devil is to refuse to believe in him has profound psychological truth. It is easy enough to identify the man who has no perception of his Shadow but less easy to notice this same deficiency in ourselves. So we should always be on guard against the tendency to locate evil outside ourselves, to be certain of our own righteousness, to put ourselves on the side of the angels in some imagined spiritual warfare. Those without shadows – or more accurately those who behave as if they are without shadows – are either maniacs or Pharisees. The identifying mark is in both cases the location of evil *somewhere else:* the religious maniac does this sensationally by announcing himself as leader of the crusade against the forces of darkness; the Pharisee is less dramatic but the soul-destroying smugness is there just the same – 'The Pharisee stood and prayed thus with himself, God I thank thee that I am not as other men are, extortioners, unjust, adulterers, or even as this publican' (Luke 18.11).

Traditionally, it is the Devil's job to subvert man's faith in God, to cause man to imagine he can get by on his own efforts. This delusion leads to damnation. In psychological terms the issue is the same, as the Shadow teaches the ego to imagine that ego is all. This leads to a denial of the archetype of the Self and to the psychological deterioration which corresponds to the traditional religious concept of damnation. A good place to see the struggle in progress is in the detailed form of Satan's temptations in St Matthew, chapter 4.

The first temptation is for Jesus to believe that he can do as he likes without reference to God. 'Command that these stones be made bread' (verse 3). Satan is trying to persuade Jesus to rely upon his own power, that is upon the ego. Jesus answers the temptation by claiming that true power and authority rests with God, '. . . by every word that proceedeth out of the mouth of God' (verse 4). And, as we know, in terms of psychological effects, God and the Self are the same. Here we see the double aspect of the Shadow's personality: he exists to subvert faith, to draw man's attention away from God, to cause man to deny his dependence upon God; but in the very process of doing this he must necessarily also direct attention towards God. This is so because of the logic of negativity. By suggesting that man should rely only upon man, Satan prompts the reply 'Man should rely upon God'. In the idea of one alternative, another alternative presents itself. 'Do this!' provokes the answer 'Why should I?' 'Choose black!' indicates that at least there is a choice. This is explained in St Paul's more abstract terminology: 'That as sin hath reigned unto death, even so might grace reign through righteousness. . .' (Rom. 5.21). Because Satan is part of God's creation, he cannot help serving God, even if he does not do so intentionally. Because the Shadow is part of the whole personality, it cannot but play its part in the integration of the personality.

In the first temptation, the Devil tries to persuade Jesus to ignore God. In the second temptation, he encourages him to misperceive God. '. . . cast thyself down: for it is written, He shall give his angels charge concerning thee: and in their hands they shall bear thee up, lest at any time thou dash thy foot against a stone' (verse 6). In the jargon of logistics, the battle has been escalated. The Devil has progressed from talking about something which a man might do to a discussion of the activity and purpose of God himself. A psychological paraphrase of the second temptation might go as follows: 'The ego can do as it pleases because it will always be preserved by the superior force of the Self'. This is an inversion of the scheme of salvation, of the true course of the individuation process. Jesus' forthright answer 'It is written again, Thou shalt not tempt the Lord thy God' is an insistence that man exists for the benefit of God and not the other way about. Man's part is to fulfil the purposes of God; it is not God's function to pander to the whims of man. Or: the ego must take its place in the totality of the

Self, for the Self is greater than the ego. This is the meaning of the saying in Luke, 'wist ye not that I must be about my Father's business?' (2.49) and of many verses in John which speak of Jesus' relationship with his Father (5.19, 37; 5.57 8.18; 12.50).

In the third temptation the attention is switched again; this time the Devil himself is the focus of interest. He has tried to get Jesus first to ignore God, then to misperceive him; now he concentrates his attention on the demonic option: 'All these things will I give thee, if thou wilt fall down and worship me' (verse 9). Of necessity this is the last temptation of the three because it assumes a certain sophistication which can have come only through experience of spiritual warfare. It takes for granted the fact that Jesus knows who the Devil is. In psychological terms, progress has been made; the ego no longer denies or projects the Shadow, but is able to identify him clearly. The Devil is Jesus' alter-ego. He is the other option, an option which consists in making material conquests rather than serving the kingdom of God. Psychologically, this is equivalent to the wish to remain engaged in conscious activities and desires alone, to refuse the invitation to dialogue and relationship with the greater forces of the unconscious.

The most strikingly positive result of the temptations is that Jesus emerges from the wilderness with his mind clear. He knows who he is and what he must do. This knowledge and insight has come about entirely through his arguments with the Devil. These arguments constitute the process of thinking and rethinking, of rejecting some valuations in favour of others. We have seen how this necessarily involves examining certain options which are well described as evil; for without an encounter with evil the individual does not remain pure, only naive. A naïve and gullible saviour is the last thing mankind needs. This encounter with the dark side of the personality is the process of self-examination, penitence and reorientation. It is not a question of grovelling, of being bogged down in a mire of guilt but of rethinking our vocation in the context of all the available points of view. The most important aspect of confession is not how bad we feel about our alleged sins, but how clearly we think about our spiritual orientation and motives. Jesus came out of the wilderness knowing his future direction. That is what we should always know after an act of confession. And as in many subsequent passages Jesus is said to have removed himself from the disciples in order to pray, so our own acts of rethinking should be frequent and progressive.

In classical spirituality it is sometimes said that the prayer of silence is superior to the prayer which uses words. There is a sense too in which a verbal, propositionalized, exchange with the Shadow is inferior and less mature than an unspoken awareness of the Shadow's existence. However, as in the case of prayer, it is necessary to go through the preliminary and elementary stages before the more advanced level is reached. There are no more accounts in the New Testament of any specific arguments between Jesus and Satan, but we may be sure that Jesus was constantly aware of Satan's presence. The dealings with evil spirits, the words to Peter after the Caesarea Philippi incident and the cry of dereliction from the cross demonstrate the truth of this. Our own task is to know our own darkness and weakness as well as we know our own strengths. Indeed to know one is to know the other. This is true progress in self-understanding. 'Better the Devil you know than the one you do not know', says the proverb. In psychological terms, knowing the Devil means being able to discriminate within the conscious and unconscious life of the psyche. In this interior struggle we begin to draw nearer to God, we see the first stages of that psychological balance and individuation which is our proper destiny. This struggle is rightly described as internal, for all the necessary characters exist within our own soul. As Meister Eckhardt says, 'You haven't got to borrow from God, for he is your own and therefore, whatever you get, you get from yourself. If a man's work is to live, it must come from the depths of him – not from alien sources outside himself – but from within.'

The question then arises of what is the nature and form of temptation not only for Jesus but for ourselves. It amounts to the same thing: the attempt to avoid or evade that meeting with God which we find painful but which our soul knows as the one thing that is necessary. The ego always resists the promptings of the larger Self precisely because the Self requires sacrifice on the part of the ego. And yet, in the last resort, the pain which follows from our refusing to find our meaning in God is infinitely more excruciating than what we suffer in seeking to avoid him. This is the meaning of all the mythological imagery about hell and the lake of fire, the inferno, the abode of the lost and so on. Only we do not really believe that our ultimate happiness is to be found in

God and instead we seek it in things – even in what we are sometimes proud to call spiritual things. If God is the real goal of all our striving, why do we resist him so fiercely? Because often when he appears he demands fundamental changes in us and we find this sort of change disturbing. The means of change is always painful reorientation, rethinking, *metanoia,* penitence. Nor are we much encouraged by progress made in the past. The struggle seems always to be uphill. The problem is always a new problem.

One way of illustrating this is the pain felt by the creative artist until he has brought forth a new and completed work. It does not matter to the novelist that he has a shelf behind his desk containing twenty first class works all written by himself; what does concern him is the empty page before him. His pain can only be arrested by filling that page (and the next and the next) with new words, with another story. As Auden said, 'The next poem is all that ever matters!' And at least one of the messages to be learned from Goethe's *Faust* is that it is the cry 'Verweile doch, du bist so schön!' (Stay thou art so fair!) which is the sign of death and sterility. The process of individuation is continuous and new problems arise every day. A new effort, similar to, but ultimately different from, the last effort is always needed. 'God is the God of the living' (Matt. 22.32). 'Behold, I make all things new' (Rev. 21.5). Confession. Rethinking. We must be born again, not once but every day.

Always this requires a step into the complete darkness of faith, even into the darkness of the absence of God. If we always knew where the spiritual life was leading us we should be in possession already of that which lies ahead. That is impossible of course for 'Faith is the substance of things hoped for, the evidence of things not seen' (Heb. 11.1). Nothing could be more direct or more explicit than this statement, and yet we do not accept it; we try instead to believe that somehow we can see what is not seen and consequently we derive only false comfort from our piety.

There is another paradox about confession which affects our whole idea of the spiritual life; we must constantly rethink our lives and always be ready to take a new step in faith, trusting in the resources of God or the Self if we are to make spiritual progress; but we should never do these things *in order* to make spiritual progress. There is an old saying to the effect that our concerns are work and charity while the salvation of our soul is God's business;

if we look after the first he will look after the second. Certainly, there is something almost disgusting about the spiritual and psychological contortions of those who are obsessed with the idea of improving themselves; and some Christians' preoccupation with individual salvation as the greatest good – or in some cases the only good – is just as unhealthy. An overriding concern for the salvation of my own soul goes completely against the spirit of Jesus. And, in psychological terms, we frequently find that such obsessions degenerate into what is morbid and psychopathological. If we insist on trying to save our lives we shall lose our lives. That, in contrast with the workings of human economy, is how the divine system functions (Matt. 10.39) I cannot imagine Jesus having many words of commendation for the activities of either those groups who gather at the ashram of the latest guru and prepare themselves to perform all manner of psychological gymnastics in order to 'get the head together', or of those so obsessed with guilt and with what they fondly imagine are their sins that they can never stop harping on these things to any audience prepared to listen. Whereas most genuine conversion stories have much to do with the painful process of rethinking rather than only feeling ashamed of a few covert indulgences. Paul's experience on the road to Damascus was the culmination of a long and strenuous process of evaluation – which is rightly called 'repentance'.

4 | Thanksgiving

We do not say thank you for God's sake, for he needs nothing from us; we say thank you for our own good. It is not as if God will be offended if we do not accord him sufficient gratitude for his mercies. When the Bible says that God gives freely, it means exactly that. He is not like a sour old aunt who gives presents only so that she can extract a word of appreciation from her nephew – or so that she herself can pronounce a note of disapproval if that appreciation is not immediately forthcoming. Genuine thanksgiving is properly more humbling than confession for it is the recognition that we are not the authors of our own being but that we experience the world, including the people in it, as *given*. I said it is humbling; and humility itself is nothing other than a true sense of perspective. It is not humble to grovel or to become so self-effacing that our personality becomes almost tenuous. It is not a question of trying to make ourselves out to be less useful, worthy or potent than we are, in the false supposition that thereby we achieve virtue. Humility is the knack of seeing ourselves as we are, and thanksgiving is a powerful help in this task.

In one sense, everything that we have and are is given. Everything is derived – material goods, family, friends, flesh and blood. Even the form of our character and intelligence is very largely fashioned for us by our genetic inheritance and our upbringing. To be thankful then is to accept experience as the raw material which has been given and upon which we must work. The image of experience as a work is to be found in many areas of life from that of the sculptor who chips away at raw material until it is given individual form, to the symbolic work of alchemy which sees salvation (pictorialized as gold) as the result of a long process of change among the primitive elements. The many different languages used to describe the process of personal development are interchangeable. Talk of God and the soul, heaven and hell is the theological equivalent of psychological jargon about the Self and the archetypes of the unconscious; and this in turn is only a linguistic variant of the alchemical vocabulary which features transmutations from nigredo to pure gold. This is not to make the story of human personality into something banal, as if it could maintain its dignity only by being limited to one language; on the contrary it is to demonstrate the significance of that story by the discovery that it turns up again and again irrespective of the vocabulary employed. We should remember also that all our language is given. This is not a trivial concept, for language of one sort or another is what we chiefly use to express all that we are and hope for.

To be thankful is to enter the meditative silence beyond language wherein we realize that everything, including language itself, is given. In the ordinary course of events, in the middle of our busy lives of planning, organizing and deciding important issues, we easily run away with the idea that we ourselves are the centre of the world; we forget that we owe our origin to others, perhaps even to Another. And to be entirely realistic we need to behave like this for much of the time. We cannot leave it to God or to the archetypes of the collective unconscious to provide for our families, to mend the hole where the slates blew off, to put out the forest fire. Nonetheless, there needs to be time for the recollection that when all is said and done we are not the originators of our own being and that there is much that is beyond our control. This can be achieved by very simple means – just saying the words of the General Thanksgiving or of some other prayer for example. This is often enough to focus our minds, to generate a sense of perspective about our own place in the order of things. But it is worth repeating that the thanksgiving is not in the words but in the sense of perspective engendered by the occasion of their utterance. So, frequently it is not direct language but oblique language which brings about the thankful disposition. If I read a Psalm or a 'secular' poem I may be stirred suddenly to see the wonder of the

world and that this is not of my making. I put down the book and
sit in silence for a few moments. That is an act of thanksgiving,
and I emerge from it with a renewed and deepened awareness of
my own place in the whole vast scheme of things; a place neither
too exalted nor too abased, the right place, a proper balance
between hubris and self-denigration. I can be proud so long as I
am not proud of my own actions but of what is being enacted in
me by all that is given:

> Verily, verily I say unto you, The Son can do nothing of himself,
> but what he seeth the Father do (John 5.19).
> Nevertheless I live: yet not I, but Christ liveth in me (Gal. 2.20).

Philosophers and poets continue to strive to achieve a true
perspective, a simple, immediate and indubitable truth which is
beyond words. Sometimes it seems as if this has been glimpsed in
mystical experience or in the inspiration of great art. Paradoxically,
as soon as the mystic, the saint or the artist begins to recount his
vision, it is no longer of transcendent (and therefore translinguistic)
status. The vision becomes encapsulated in a story or in a picture
and, glorious though it may be, it is immediately susceptible to
interpretation and criticism. It is easy to understand why we
sometimes become angry when others try to interpret religious
imagery, and especially when scholars criticize biblical narrative;
we feel that an outrage is being committed against what is sacred,
transcendent, above words and therefore beyond criticism. But we
are wrong to be angry, because no representation of intuited truth
is beyond interpretation, comment and criticism. To make it so is
to make an idol. Indeed, the mystic or the prophet in the very act
of describing his vision is himself taking part in the activity of
commentary and criticism. His *account* is not sacred; only that
beyond, that *given* of which it is an account is sacred. Man's proper
response to religious experience, to what is given, is awe and
thanksgiving. Thanksgiving often takes the form of spontaneous
creative expression and, at its highest, this is great religious art
whether the object of thanksgiving appears to be particularly
religious or not. In this sense all art is religious because, whatever
its form, the motivation behind it is to express the inexpressible.
The true artist is never satisfied; that is, he refuses to become an
idolater, to stay fixated on one expression of his vision. To repeat
Auden's words, 'The next poem is all that ever matters'. But we

do not have to be great artists in order to give new thanks for 'new mercies each returning day'.

There is one particular area of prayer in which thanksgiving finds its special place and that is to do with the sacraments. These have power and influence beyond the limits of language and they support language in the way that the bank guarantees the value of currency. Just as the tribesman begins his ritual dance in order to bring about some hoped for state of affairs, or as the child starts her rhyming incantation in the playground ignorant of the cognitive meaning of her words, so the groom gives his bride a ring as a translinguistic pledge, as a 'token and pledge' of his commitment. The Prayer Book insists that man and woman are joined together in Holy Matrimony as much by 'the giving and receiving of a ring and by joining of hands' as by the verbal promises made. Similarly, baptismal promises are not complete without water. Confirmation and Ordination require the laying on of hands. Supremely, Communion is by bread and wine.

Millions of words have been written about the theology of sacraments, about the grace that is conferred by them, whether this is objective or subjective, whether Christ's presence is 'real' in the sacred elements, whether we should define the mode of his presence as 'transubstantiation' (Aquinas) or as 'transignification' (Schillebeeckx). It is beyond the scope of this chapter to join these controversies. All I am trying to point to here is the translinguistic, given, nature of sacramental objects and their connection with the spiritual and psychological disposition of thankfulness. In particular I want to suggest that, whatever other deep and subtle truths there may be in the doctrine of the Holy Eucharist (the Thanksgiving), there is a powerful and creative spiritual usefulness involved in seeing it as a gratuitous act. ('Gratuitous' – got or given free, not earned or paid for, uncalled for, unwarranted etc: *The Concise Oxford Dictionary*.) The sacrament or gift of the bread and wine reminds us of the given-ness of the world. Whatever is said about these elements – even whatever is written about them! – they are simply *there* and their function is simply *to be* there. They are a sign which tells man that he must take the world on trust. There are limits to language, even to religious language. When we have used our intellects thoroughly in the attempt to understand the scriptures in the Holy Communion, we come to the altar in order to receive that which goes beyond the definitions of intellect.

We receive and we give thanks. Our thanksgiving is for the existence of the world which makes possible all our experience. But we do not give thanks only for an object or even for that set of objects which constitutes the world; we give thanks for the revelation in Christ that the world is of a particular moral nature. In the sacrament of the bread and the wine, as in all the other sacraments, fact and value, essence and significance are combined.

Following Christ's command, we 'this do in remembrance of (him)' (Luke 22.19). This is no mere memorial but a real proclamation of Christ. In taking the bread and wine we affirm that the whole of existence is defined by the life and death of Christ. In this sense he is the Way, the Truth and the only Life that is possible for all men (John 14.6). By taking the bread and wine we accept the life of Christ as the pattern for our own lives and the way he lived as the way for ourselves. This is not slavish copying, aping a moral teacher long since dead; it is the perception, understanding and acceptance of what it means to be a man. It is also the meaning of the text:

> Neither is there salvation in any other; for there is none other name under heaven given among men, whereby we must be saved (Acts 4.12).

What we are affirming in the act of communion is the inevitability of Christ's destiny for us also. And any attempt to live otherwise leads only to spiritual and psychological chaos, to what the New Testament calls 'death'. The fact is of course that we make many such evasive attempts because, on the face of it, the pattern of Christ's life does not appear as enviable. But there is no avoiding it, for it is the truth.

I do not wish to appear so narrow-minded as to suggest that we can live this life only in and through the church. The church gives a traditional expression and interpretation of this life in its sacraments and doctrines, in the regular and systematic reading of the gospel story; and this whole scheme provides a frame of reference which is intellectually and emotionally coherent. The universal archetypes are given particular reference as we read of Christ's birth, his baptism, suffering, death and resurrection. A man who has no connection with the church may, or even must, live according to this pattern; but if he does not avail himself of the scheme which the church provides, he is almost certain to find himself having to invent some other terminology in which to understand and describe his experience. Only the experience does not vary between the churched and the unchurched; everyone, whether he likes it or not, must live and suffer and die. And if a man becomes an atheistic humanist or else an existentialist, he still cannot escape from the truth which is written on his own soul or, in the language of psychology, in the structure of his psyche. So he will invent another myth within which to understand his experience, but the same problems will remain: how to deal with anxiety and suffering; the relationship with my neighbour; the inevitability of death and so on. Ideological differences, how ever strongly expressed, do not go very deep; they are differences in what Wittgenstein called 'surface grammar' rather than in 'depth grammar'. Our depth grammar is all of a piece because we all share the same basic experiences. This is certainly true within the Western tradition where basic values scarcely vary among theists and atheists, 'religious' and 'secular'. If there were profound differences, these would soon become apparent in widely differing patterns of behaviour. But what do we see? That socialist ethics is a kind of demythologized form of Christian morality, that the existentialist is also in bondage to sin, though he calls it 'angst' and that, as Russell pointed out, the communist has completely remythologized his outlook on the same underlying structure as that of Christian eschatology. And recent study of world religions has shown that there is a great measure of agreement on the deepest issues even between civilizations and creeds which were once considered irredeemably at odds. The essence of thanksgiving, therefore, is not merely an acknowledgment that we are not the authors of our own being, but that the being we share is of a type and universality which we see particularized in Jesus. Paul said, 'We preach Christ crucified, unto the Jews a stumbling block and unto the Greeks foolishness' (I Cor. 1.23). And there are the equals of Jews and Greeks in the modern world: among them Don Cupitt for whom the story of the crucifixion is a great stumbling block, 'a story that cannot be told' because it contains 'morally repellent symbolism'. But a story which purports to be the truth about men *must* contain morally repellent symbolism because men's lives are full of morally repellent facts. Cupitt and liberal theologians like him, heirs to the Marcionite heresy, would banish evil from the cosmos by strenuous labours, by purifying our religious consciousness and by generally looking on the bright side; well-intentioned though they might be, the truth is that evil cannot be got rid of in this way since men's souls (psyches) are made up of darkness and light. Any programme therefore, religious or political, which does not take account of the real existence of evil is bound to prove inadequate to the experience of mankind. Spiritual (psychological) evil is ever present. It is there in the crucifixion. It is there also in wars and violence, in greed and hatred, in all the sordid and petty acts of selfishness and indulgence which ruin personal relationships. That is the relevance of Paul's preaching. That is why the most powerful symbol is the cross.

Thanksgiving is not politely expressed gratitude for goodies – 'All good gifts around us are sent from heaven above', so where do the bad gifts come from? – it is the acknowledgment of a given-ness which includes suffering. And to thank God is to accept the fundamental rightness of this revelation, to accept it not just in the life of Jesus and in the ornaments of the church but as the truth about our own lives as well. We must, if we are to thank God at all, thank him for what he is and not for what we might, in our shallower moments when we talk of morally repellent symbolism, rather like him to be. Or, in other words, if we are to accept life, we must show acceptance for life as it is, for the whole creation, and not just for those parts of it which we find pleasant or amusing. To perceive God falsely is either idolatry or heresy; to turn one's back on disturbing aspects of experience is hypocrisy or neurosis. However, thanksgiving is not quietism. It does not say that so long as evil exists there is nothing that can be done about it; but that evil cannot be lightly dismissed or dispersed by the religion of healthy-mindedness and a naïve trust in progress and education; evil can be overcome only by being accepted and transformed. That is the message of the cross and it is as true for social and political evils as it is for the tensions existing in man's own individual psychological make up.

5 | Supplication

We do not make supplicatory prayers so that God will give us what we want, but we pray that our will may be conformed to his will. A truism, but one that is not given complete emotional acceptance. Every week we hear churchmen pray for peace – not as for a spiritual gift but as if they really expected God to intervene in the wars between the Jews and the Arabs and even in the internecine strife which might exist between, say, the NUR and ASLEF. Intercessions in church usually sound like the itinerary of a global trip with stops off at resorts favoured by the intercessor. 'For peace with justice in Southern Africa, in Argentina in the Middle-East; and for all men persecuted for their beliefs especially . . .' Here insert either 'Russian dissidents' or 'the poor and dispossessed in Brazil' depending upon whether the intercessor derives his political views from *The Guardian* or from the *Daily Telegraph*. Rarely will you hear *both* clauses, both sides of the ideological divide prayed for.

In fact, most Christians do not now believe that God can be regarded as a conveniently omnipotent efficient cause; so his efforts are not called upon to provide a fine day for the Garden Party or a parking spot for the Vicar when he arrives at the hospital to do his sick visiting. Most people would regard these sorts of prayers as indicators of a naïve and misleading opinion about God's agency in the world. But still we hear prayers in church – and perhaps we even pray them privately – which involve this misleading view. It is as if we were to believe that the justice or importance of the cause for which we pray somehow justifies the entirely naïve prayer. We are embarrassed at prayers for parking spaces but we feel it is right to pray for peace in the Middle East or on the railways. But the two sets of prayers are exactly similar in form and we are in both cases asking for supernatural intervention – asking God to do something. Whereas, we should remember the truism with which we began, the truism taught to all confirmation candidates. Supplicatory prayer is designed not to alter God's will but to conform our wills to his.

Why is it wrong to ask God to do things for us? Is it always wrong to pray in this way? I believe that the answer depends entirely on our own motives; there are a number of reasons why it is wrong to pray for God to do something, and there is one reason why it is entirely right to do so. First the wrong reasons.

Intercessory prayer that concentrates on specific events and issues is often dishonest and unfair. There was an old film about the Second World War and in it two British airmen were praying for a fine day for their bombing mission while German airmen were praying for cloudy weather. As if to point up the absurdity of this, the film script included the lines 'It makes you wonder whose side God is on!' These lines were spoken first by the Germans and then by the British. Was God supposed to listen to the prayers of both sides and then weigh the arguments carefully before creating the weather? And if so, on what basis was he supposed to make his decision in the end? This is a deliberately stark example but it shows clearly how intercessory prayer of this sort produces the absurd concept of a partisan deity. For example, what sort of prayers should have been prayed at the time of the Falklands War? I suggest that the following clauses were all logically and morally possible:

   (i) That our forces should achieve a quick and, so far as the sacrifice of lives is concerned, a cheap victory.
  (ii) (i) prayed by Argentinians.
 (iii) That we should withdraw our forces and tolerate the status quo in the Falklands.
 (iv) (iii) prayed by Argentinians.
  (v) That there should be a just and lasting peace – prayed by British, Argentinians and third parties all over the world.

Clearly prayers (i)–(iv) are no different in form and structure from the prayers of the airmen in the film; they amount to rival petitions requiring God to perform contradictory acts. Thus they are absurd. But prayer (v) is only more of the same sort of thing. For who is to decide what would constitute 'a just and lasting peace'? Obviously there would be a great difference of opinion between the British and the Argentinians; and third parties might harbour a dozen or more opinions about what is just in the circumstances. So when the intercessor steps out into the aisle to pray for this just and lasting peace, it follows that he is doing one of two things: either, he already has in his mind what constitutes justice in this affair – in which case we are simply back among prayers of the (i)–(iv) variety; or else he does not know what would constitute such a just outcome and he is therefore prepared to leave the matter in God's hands – in which case he must simply accept that *whatever happens* is just. The only alternative is that God has ignored his prayer and allowed injustice to triumph. But if God is so capricious as to allow injustice to triumph, then what use are all our prayers? If he is not capricious but merely unable to prevent the triumph of injustice, then once again what is the use of praying? We are left in the old dilemma about whether God is just but not all-powerful or whether he is all-powerful but unjust. In either case he is not the sort of God anyone could pray to with confidence. So prayer (v), the bland catch-all of the politically 'moderate', is as naïve and even as dishonest as prayers of the (i)–(iv) variety. The intercessor's vagueness might save the appearances and allow room for the different opinions to be found among his congregation, but the price paid is the forfeit of sense and reason. Prayer (v) is either incoherent and open to contradictory interpretation – which a cynic might argue it was always meant to be – or else it is as partisan and morally cocksure as prayers (i)–(iv).

A more general objection to this sort of motivation behind prayers of supplication involves the way in which we think of the being of God himself. I think it is always a mistake to regard God as an efficient cause. I do not believe that he polishes the stars every daytime so that they will shine all the more brightly at night, nor that he causes the planets to complete their orbits. Stark examples once again, but more refined descriptions of God's work as an efficient cause contain the same difficulties. Either we can measure God's activity as an efficient cause or we cannot measure it. If we can measure the activity then there is no way of telling the

difference between an efficient cause which is God and a thousand
other efficient causes which are not God. In short, if we can *ever
detect* God's activity in the world, then it is no longer the activity
of a supernatural and transcendent being, simply because anything
that can be detected must be natural, by definition. If, on the other
hand, we cannot detect God's activity in the world, then all our
statements about God as efficient cause are quite meaningless. If
we cannot detect his activity, how do we ever know that he has
acted?

Suppose there is a third alternative. Suppose that in some way
that is quite beyond our powers of understanding God yet acts as
efficient cause and actual sustainer of the universe. The question
immediately arises: why is he so bad at the job? An almighty
efficient cause could surely prevent earthquakes and tidal waves;
surely he could moderate extreme temperatures and climates so
that there were not vast areas of waste in the world; surely he could
avert the meaningless and unearned suffering that happens not
infrequently to embryos and children.

We are once again faced with the two unsatisfactory answers of
either that he cannot do these things or that he chooses not to do
them. In the first case he is not almighty while in the second case
he is unjust.

Now I would like to try and discuss the idea of supplicatory
prayer in a way which does not involve these unsolvable problems.
I am not trying to destroy the notion of supplication and with it
the whole idea of God. I am trying to remove what I believe to be
a false and therefore misleading way of thinking about God. So
long as we maintain that he is an efficient cause – a God who acts
in the same way that men act though on an infinitely larger scale
– we are bound to run into difficulties which are insurmountable.
I want to remove what I believe to be a misleading idea of God so
that a more helpful idea of him might emerge. Wittgenstein is
famous for having said that 'philosophical problems arise when
language goes on holiday' and that we must constantly battle
against 'the bewitchment of our intelligence by the use of language'.
I believe all those images of God as efficient cause lead only to the
bewitchment of our thought about him and eventually to an
inability to make sense of the idea of God at all. That is the only
reason why they should be removed. There is no way of talking to,
say, the mother of a child born blind and crippled, about that sort

of God – no way that is not incoherent and so finally implausible. But there is another sense of God, a sense shared by the classical mystics and by modern analytical psychologists, which might eventually be of some help to that woman, to her child and to anyone else who seeks to pursue it.

This view of God sees him not as efficient cause but as final cause. He is not our maker in that he made us out of nothing but he is our maker and our goal in the sense that he draws us to him. God is our purpose. He is the one to whom we tend. Earlier in the discussion we saw how it is the destiny of the ego to be subordinate to the Self, to allow itself to be shaped by the influence of the Self; we saw how this works inwardly in the process of psychological integration as life progresses. We saw the example of its working in the story of Jesus when he prays, 'O my Father, if it be possible, let this cup pass from me: nevertheless not as I will, but as thou wilt' (Matt. 26.29). This is the pattern of the will's obedience to a higher will. Man's obedience to God. The ego's subordination to that whole which is called the Self. As a guide to all our views about the purpose and value of supplicatory prayer, we might take that saying of Jesus in two parts and ask which was the greater prayer 'let this cup pass' or 'not as I will, but as thou wilt'? Unquestionably, we answer, the second prayer. This then is the example for us, the true definition of all supplicatory prayer: our will must be conformed to the will of God. Or, in psychological terms, the narrow and immediate wishes of the ego must be made subordinate to the individuating presence of the whole Self. This is always true. It is the life of faith itself – the willingness to admit and to obey, to submit and to follow even when these acts seem to be the very last things likely to contribute to our soul's well-being.

This has all been about the *theory* of supplicatory prayer but tangible results come from its *practice* and I would like to turn now to some of these. First, supplicatory prayer is an important means by which we come to see what the will of God is – or, in terms that might prove acceptable to those who still feel squeamish at the word 'God', by which we come to see which things are morally inevitable. For instance, it is only after Christ has prayed that the cup pass from him that he discovers it to be God's will that the cup should not pass from him. So when we pray for anything, we expose our own will our own motives in the very act of praying. I am rightly embarrassed if I catch myself praying for a parking place; and eventually, through the regular practice of supplicatory prayer, I am able to evaluate all my motives and desires in the same way and to begin to reject all those aspects which are unworthy – the will of man or ego-seeking – and instead conform my will to the will of God, to what is morally inevitable. I suggest that this is no watered-down or inferior view of the purpose of supplicatory prayer to that view criticized in the first part of this section. On the contrary, it is a view supported by mystical theologians down the centuries and also by the practical discoveries of analytical psychology. True supplication does not aim at changing God but at converting man. It does not seek the ends of the fragmented and partisan ego but of the greater unity which is called the Self.

Secondly, supplication is the beginning of charity in that it makes us conscious of others. By praying for others, or by calling to mind their needs and concerns, their needs and concerns become mine as well. And supplication often leads to very practical assistance. If I pray for someone I am the more likely to try and do something within my power to help him. The parable of the vineyard, in which one of the sons promises to go and work for his father but does not go, reveals the hypocrisy and futility of prayer without action, of words without corresponding deeds – where deeds are possible (Matt. 21. 28–31). And yet supplication can be of value even where we can do nothing else, for it brings home to us through the rehearsal of others' needs our kinship with all men, our shared creatureliness. For what has unhappily befallen *Thou* might easily have been something in which *I* was involved. Indeed it is the prayer of supplication which shows me that I am involved whether I am aware of the fact or not. John Donne's 'ask not for whom the bell tolls; it tolls for thee', and 'Inasmuch as ye have done it unto one of the least of these my brethren, ye have done it unto me' (Matt. 25.40) are both saying the same thing.

Thirdly, supplicatory prayers help root the spiritual life very firmly in the everyday world. It is tempting – as it was tempting for the disciples at the Transfiguration – to try to live on an exalted spiritual plane all the time. If we are not wary, we can fall in love with the words of spiritual counsellors and with the states described by them, so that spirituality itself becomes a sort of drug. We can become proud of our ability to think and talk about the means of salvation; we can imagine ourselves to be on nodding terms with the archetypes of the collective unconscious. Supplication reminds us that our task is in this world and that it involves dealings even (especially) with those people whom we might regard as rather tedious and mundane in our lofty flights of fancy. The mystics describe spirituality as a work and it is a work which needs constant and close attention; they also insisted that it has both outer and inner aspects which complement each other. And we can learn much from the ancient injunction that, if while at our prayers we hear our neighbour call out for help, then we are to leave our prayers and attend first to the needs of our neighbour. There is no psychological jargon so sublime that it removes from us responsibilities touching the needs of others. By another paradox of faith we shall also find that by attending to our neighbour we have attended to our own soul. But, as in the issue of personal salvation, we should not so attend *in order that* we might achieve benefit ourselves. The tyranny of the ego knows no bounds especially in those issues which are connected with virtue and with doing good! Supplication is a principal method of setting a watch over the ego, of joining our will to the will of God.

IV BEING GOOD: A PRELUDE TO MORALS

1 | Grace and Faith

If Christ had issued any commandments, his message to mankind would not have been formally different from the Ten Commandments or any other moral code. The difference between Christian ethics and any other moral code is that all the moral codes tell us what to do in order to be good, to act justly, to achieve virtue and so on, while Christian ethics begins from the premise that man can only very rarely, if ever, act justly. Christian ethics is based on Christian psychology which takes the view that there is a double aspect to man's personality; he is made in the image of God *and* his heart inclines towards evil. This spiritual or psychological judgment is given expression in all Jesus' parables about men with two sons (Matt. 21.28; Luke 15.11, etc.) and in the characterization of Jesus' own encounter with Satan. In this matter, Christian ethics is entirely realistic. It does not expect from man more than he is able to give, but provides a radical solution to the problem of how a man is to fulfil his desire to live with integrity when he knows he is unable to do this. Paul puts this plainly at the beginning of his epistle to the Romans: 'For as many as have sinned without law shall also perish without law: and as many as have sinned in the law shall be judged by the law' (2.12). 'For all have sinned, and come short of the glory of God' (3.23). Therefore, if we are to be saved, to achieve moral integrity, it cannot be by our own doing, it must be by grace. In New Testament terms grace is the act of God towards man and man's response is faith. Our task then is to try to understand what is meant by 'grace' and 'faith'.

There have been many attempts to define grace, including the doctrine of grace as *ex opere operato*, the so-called tap-water theory which sees grace mediated by the sacraments almost as if it were a physical substance such as water. I do not think that this view is particularly helpful in an age when all our thinking about the mediation of spiritual qualities has been changed by the way we construe physical science. There is a valid way of seeing the sacraments as means of grace and that is to regard these as signs of the given-ness of experience. To receive a sacrament is to be in the watershed between the past and the future and to know where you are. Received after proper preparation, a sacrament is a sign that the past is gone and that a future of new possibility – the famous 'clean slate' – is available. It might be helpful to picture grace as that new possibility. This is the message of Jesus: 'Go and sin no more' (John 8.11). But, of course, Jesus needs to say those words to us every day, because we do sin again and again. Spiritually, he does say them and grace makes possible innumerable new beginnings in which we stand uncondemned. In psychological terms, grace means the resources of the Self made available to the ego. These resources, like God's grace in the old language, are always available and this means that, whatever the spiritual or psychological conflict within the individual, the power exists within that same individual to resolve it. Just as God is defined as transcendent, so grace, in psychological terms, is the property or function of the unconscious. It exists to resolve conscious crises and to bring wholeness (salvation – individuation) to the personality. The good news of the New Testament is that God does not accuse us or condemn us; he forgives. Similarly the Self is always able to accommodate ego and shadow in a unity which neither ego nor shadow by themselves could bring about. Thus the ego is dependent on the Self as man is dependent upon God. It is a question only of which language is preferred when discussing immediate spiritual or psychological experiences. We may reject God or the archetype of the Self, but we are unable to deny the experiences themselves; and, if both God and the Self are rejected, then a new language will have to be found. So the Marxist talks about 'alienation' and the existentialist invents the phrase 'inauthentic existence' where the Bible speaks of 'sin'. There follow 'liberation', 'authenticity', 'salvation' and so on – words to cover every category of inner experience. It would take an infinite series of books to compare the ways in which our experience is notated and described in all the different religious and ideological languages; for the purposes of this book I think it wise to limit myself to two such systems – Christian theology and the language of analytical psychology. But we should remember that these are not the only representations available.

As for 'faith', there has been more controversy about this word than about any other term used in Christian theology. Sometimes the New Testament texts do not seem to be very helpful. Paul says, 'Therefore we conclude that a man is justified by faith. . .' (Rom. 3.28) while James says, 'Faith without works is dead' (James 2.17). The issue is complicated by theologians who claim that faith itself is a work. However, if we are not capable of saving ourself by our own goodness – if, that is, the ego cannot achieve wholeness without a relationship with the Self – it follows that faith must be more in the nature of what *happens* to us rather than something which we *do*. If it were something done by us, then it would be a work. The doctrine of justification by faith, the core of Christian morality, explicitly denies that we can do anything to save ourselves. So it is singularly unhelpful to tell someone in one breath that he can do nothing to save himself, but in the next breath to tell him to have faith. The moral theologian Geoffrey Allen put this contradiction nicely when he said, in the course of criticizing a typical approach of revivalism, 'You can *do* nothing to save your soul, so now get down on your knees and *say* this. As if saying were not doing! As if speech were not an action!' Christian ethics insists that man cannot pull himself up by his boot-laces in this way; that is its whole point as well as its originality compared with other ethical systems.

I remember going, as a boy, to a radio relay in Leeds Town Hall of one of Billy Graham's sermons and being much moved by what I heard. So at the end, when he appealed to members of the congregation to come to the front and give their lives to Christ, I went forward. Afterwards, sitting at a card table with one of the team of counsellors, I was given a wallet of Bible texts of the 'wherewithal shall a young man cleanse his way . . .' variety and told to examine my life for bad habits and to stop doing them. This provoked much guilt and unhappiness in me over the next few months because of course I could not give up all my bad habits. I would try and, after holding out for a while. I would give in – only to be filled with remorse and self-hate. It never occurred to me to reflect that the counsellor had asked me to do exactly what I could not do – to save myself by my own moral effort. Whereas, the good news is, of course, that what I cannot do for myself, Christ does on my account. God does not condemn but he forgives. All I need to do is to accept his forgiveness. That really is all there is to it. Christian ethics, whatever that counsellor and many of his latter day successors might say, is not about striving to be good, to give up fags and masturbation and to try and feel right about God and my neighbour; if it were about striving to be good, then it would be justification by works and not by faith. Justification by works, by keeping the moral code, is exactly what Christianity denies in the name of its own doctrine of man's nature as fundamentally flawed.

Faith then is no sort of action. It is the refusal to try to take action. It is the rejection of all forms of striving after moral goodness in the hope that I might thereby be saved. It is the acceptance of salvation as God's 'free gift' (Rom. 5.18). None of this is to say that we should not try to be good. What, after all, would be the alternative – to try to be bad? That could never become any sort of moral principle. Nor could an impotent amoralism which does not accept any distinction between good and evil. Paul preached the doctrine of justification by faith. He was against the idea that we are saved by our striving; after all the striving he had been through as a devout Jew he knew what he was talking about. This is how he put the question: 'What shall we say then? Shall we continue in sin that grace may abound?' (Rom. 6.1). In other words, if salvation is not about moral worth but about forgiveness, then why not sin all the more so that we might receive even more forgiveness? His answer was that we are 'dead to sin' (Rom. 6.2).

Being dead to sin means that we are no longer under its power. In psychological terms, once we have seen the Shadow for what it is and acknowledged its part in us, then we are no longer living the life of damaging ignorance which comes through not recognizing our own dark side. We all know just how damaging this can be in the form of the evil we project on to others and in the delusions which we harbour about our own goodness. Being dead to sin, perceiving the shadow for what it is – these things alter the whole balance of our personality. Through these revelations we know that the way we were accustomed to act and to dispose ourself in the past does not lead to salvation or psychological wholeness. So we shall more readily act in a different way. But, because the Shadow is always part of us – because in this life we retain the capacity for sin – we shall fall away from the right path. Paul knew all about that experience too: 'For the good that I would I do not: but the evil which I would not, that I do' (Rom. 7.19). And Paul had had his Damascus Road conversion of course before he wrote those words. The fact was that he knew he still committed evil acts even after he had turned to Christ. He bewails the fact because, having seen clearly the true economy of salvation, he knows just how destructive the world of sin, that shadow-world, can be. But Paul does not make the mistake of thinking that what could not save him *before* his conversion (i.e. his own good works) can bring about his salvation *after* his conversion. The conversion showed him the deadness of sin – the unproductive chaos and ignorance of the Shadow – denying ego – but it did not and could not ensure that he would never sin again.

Faith then is not a work; it is not striving for moral worth; it is not trying to raise oneself by one's own bootstraps. Faith is not a matter of believing certain propositions about God and the historical person of Jesus Christ. It is not a matter of doctrine, any more than it is a matter of necessity for a sick man to become a medical expert in order to have his health restored. He can leave such professional considerations in the hands of his doctors. Faith is the passive acceptance of the truth that we do not need to crave justification, for we are already justified. When Paul tells us that salvation is God's 'free gift' he means exactly that; there can be no question of earning a gift. Whereas, it is sin which has its 'wages'. In psychological terms, all this means that the ego, our conscious mind, aware of its weaknesses and accepting responsibility for its Shadow, need not fall into despair and self-loathing. We are imperfect. We are even foul. But the imperfection will be coped with and fully accepted by the unconscious forces which we designate by the word 'Self'. In the old language, our imperfections are made good by the grace of God. This is the good news. It is the only good news that is possible for man in his imperfection; for all injunctions to strive only provoke even more despair when the striving fails. No wonder men are frequently exultant when the real nature of this good news dawns on them! It really is as wonderful as that. We should try to do what is right, but our salvation does not depend upon it – not in the least. No wonder also that Paul was angry with those who tried to lay moral obligations belonging to the old law on those who were newly converted.

We are called to live our lives in the knowledge that we are by grace forgiven unconditionally. This has consequences for our treatment of others. In the Lord's Prayer it says, 'And forgive us our debts as we forgive our debtors' (Matt. 6.12). It is made clear that Matthew thinks this to be the most important clause in the prayer because, after the 'Amen', he puts into the mouth of Jesus the words: 'For if ye forgive men their trespasses, your heavenly Father will also forgive you: But if ye forgive not men their trespasses, neither will your Father forgive your trespasses' (Matt. 6.14–15). In other words, the only proper attitude for a Christian towards those who have wronged him is forgiveness. How could it be otherwise? Since all have sinned and fallen short of God's glory, all are in the same state of moral helplessness. Everyone depends upon grace and forgiveness. There is no man who has the moral right therefore to judge his neighbour or to censure him. This would be possible only where the judge was perfect. Since none of us is perfect, the pseudo-ethical sanctimoni-ousness of the scribes is forbidden for us also.

But here is another paradox: if we are forgiven because we forgive, it begins to look as if our forgiveness is earned after all – by the act of forgiving others. However, since in fact we find it very difficult to exercise forgiveness, and yet the good news is that we are forgiven unconditionally – forgiven even for being unforgiving! – there can be no question of our earning salvation by any means. Those verses about forgiveness following the Lord's Prayer are like those other verses in the Sermon on the Mount which define the moral character of the inhabitants of God's kingdom; they are paradoxical in their idealism and serve to remind us that, when it comes to everyday living, we find it no easier to forgive than we find it to be pure in heart or poor in spirit. Once again, the intention of the gospel writer – like Paul's intention in the letter to the Romans – is to show us that no one is justified before God. No one is worthy. No one can become worthy, not by following Christian virtues any more than by following the commandments of biblical or natural law. The teaching of Christ is the great leveller; we are all morally helpless; our salvation consists entirely and only in recognizing that fact.

Of course, we should try to exercise Christian virtues such as forgiveness; but we can never be saved by our efforts because these efforts will always fall short of perfection. The only possible attitude therefore is that of the publican in the temple: 'God be merciful to me a sinner' (Luke 18.13); any more than this is an attempt at self-justification. It is by grace that we realize this truth. By grace we become aware from time to time that our condemnation of others' sinfulness is prohibited by our own imperfection. By grace we come to see ourselves as we are. In psychological language, it is the unconscious forces working for the wholeness of the personality which check the ego in its tendency to project its own dark side on to others. That is the meaning of the saying, 'Or how wilt thou say to thy brother, let me pull out the mote out of thine eye; and behold a beam is in thine own?' (Matt. 7.4). The injunction is to forgive our brothers 'seventy times seven' times (Matt. 8.22), in other words an infinite number of times; because we ourselves need constantly to be forgiven.

Despite all our weaknesses, the Christian ideal of morality remains and we must try to live up to it though we fail. We must try because the attempt itself is the logical consequence of the fact that we are forgiven. I mean, since we are forgiven, what else *should* we do except try to forgive others? What other moral injunction could there possibly be except, 'Be ye therefore perfect, even as your Father which is in heaven is perfect' (Matt. 5.48)? No one could make a moral imperative out of 'Be ye fairly good'. Morality must always command perfect morality. The difference between the old dispensation and the new is that whereas the old puts sinners under condemnation, the new dispensation pronounces the outrageous fact that we are forgiven. Though we are imperfect, we are treated as if we were perfect. Psychologically speaking, this means that the integrating forces of the personality, and especially the Self, are always able to cope with the errors of conscious life committed by the ego. Of course, it helps if the ego is at least aware of its errors, though it can hardly avoid error. This is the same thing that finds expression in the religious language which says we should acknowledge our transgressions (I John 1.8–9). Jung has said that the individuation process, the living development by which the personality achieves equilibrium, happens naturally and unconsciously in the majority of cases. But where the individual is aware of this process, there will occur all manner of insights and intuitions. It is the difference between mere consciousness and self-consciousness, between simply being and reflection on our being. In religious terms this means the same as the doctrine that we are all saved, whether or not we know that we are, but that those who reflect upon the manner and mode of salvation may discover truths that prove helpful to others. And this is the rôle of the priest and the spiritual guide, the pastoral counsellor and the psychotherapist. This has been the rôle of religious teachers down the centuries and particularly of Jesus Christ who had so much Self-consciousness (knowledge of God and nearness to him) that he not only proclaimed the way but, in the manner of his living, he *was* the way.

Let us take some of the Christian precepts and see how they work out their consequences in the lives of those who, however imperfectly, aim to live them. It is a fact of experience that the capacity to forgive arouses in the one who forgives a heightened sense of his own pardon. It is an inner spiritual and psychological truth that the man who is able to forgive himself thereby acts more positively towards his personal integration than the man who is bogged down in self-loathing. A constant bewailing and wringing one's hands over the fact of one's sinfulness is as negative and self-defeating a pastime as that opposite delusion of imagining that one is without sin. The Christian simply accepts the fact that he is forgiven and gets on with the task of following Christ. In psychological terms, we must learn that we can never become separated from that Shadow; ego and shadow together then must find their place in the greater integration which comes through the encounter of all the forces of the personality, conscious and unconscious. The man who either does not know his failings or who feels excessively constrained by them is like a blind man. Always his moral and spiritual progress is held up by the fact that he does not truly know where he is moving *from*. The image he has of himself is unrealistic. Jesus was united with his shadow until the cry of dereliction. Paul retained his thorn in the flesh despite the spiritual exultation which he experienced at other times. It is not going beyond the scriptural evidence to say that Paul also remained irascible, insistent to the point of pig-headedness about the rightness of his own particular interpretation of the gospel and

that he did not have a very liberal attitude towards other views –
no more than Jesus had a liberal attitude to the scribes. The life of
Jesus is not thereby undermined. The teaching of Paul is not
rendered worthless because of his faults. In fact, to return to the
subject of the Shadow's positive rôle, it is much to be doubted
whether a more 'perfect' Paul would ever have come to learn and
to experience the reality of the doctrine which he communicated
in his Epistles. That doctrine of justification was hammered out
in his own personality where the opposite forces of ego and Shadow
were forced finally to come to terms. If Jesus and Paul could not
evade these spiritual tensions, we can hardly hope to be spared
them.

2 | Loving our enemies, within and without

The definitive Christian moral principle is 'Love your enemies' (Matt. 5.44). What can this mean? First, it could never mean, 'Have a certain *feeling* about your enemies'. That is, it could never be a commandment to have a particular emotion called 'love'; for it is impossible to command emotions. Secondly, we see that something odd in terms of practical consequences seems to happen if we love our enemies. For the definition of any enemy is someone who is not loved. Therefore, if we love our enemies, we do not in fact have any enemies. I am convinced that this is part of the ironic aspect of Jesus' teaching by which he drew attention in a startling way to all the attitudes which are commonly held about personal relationships. Much of his teaching is deliberately ironic in the same way. For example, 'Blessed are they that mourn: for they shall be comforted' (Matt. 5.4). Since 'blessed' means 'happy' and to mourn is to be sad, it is clear that some ironic and paradoxical sense is intended. The same is true of 'Blessed are the meek: for they shall inherit the earth' (Matt. 5.5). In everyday experience it is Pilate and Caesar or the President of the USA, the directors of huge multinational companies and so on who inherit the earth – people with whom we do not readily associate the concept of meekness. By saying the very opposite of what is usually the case, Jesus causes his hearers to think again and to revalue those things that they have hitherto regarded as important.

Psychologists know that those who do not mourn suffer the greatest psychological damage; for it is *through* mourning and not

by trying to avoid it, that acceptance comes. And there is a deep
sense in which the meek and humble man inherits the earth in a
way that the politician and the tycoon never can. The meek person,
because he is meek, has a true perspective on the world and his
own place in it; whereas the so called 'man of power' never
discovers that perspective because he tries only to manipulate
what he sees of the world so that he may achieve his own ends.
The 'man of power' and of false perspective – the man whom Jesus
would have become had he fallen to the temptation 'All these
things will I give thee, if thou wilt fall down and worship me'
(Matt. 4.9) – manipulates while the man of meekness and humility
contemplates. And he has in his contemplation what the manipulator of material wealth can never have; for to be a manipulator a
man must believe in the real value of what he manipulates – there
was, as it were, never a miser who did *not* love money. And the
man who sets store by material things as those that are most
important, is not only liable to be disappointed when his dealings
fail, he is also wrong in his basic calculations. That is also the
meaning of, 'which of you by taking thought can add one cubit
into his stature?' (Matt. 6.27) and of the warning about laying up
treasure where the moths and rust can get at it (Matt. 6.19–20).
In all these things Jesus proclaims a revolutionary irony – revolutionary because his paradoxical words call forth exactly that
radical rethinking and reorientation which the New Testament
calls 'repentance'.

We can see also the individual psychological reference for these
sayings. 'Love your enemies' is a definition of what should be our
attitude to the Shadow, while meekness indicates the proper
disposition for the ego before the unifying agency of the Self. Again,
both outwardly in the 'moral' universe and inwardly in the
'spiritual' domain 'Love your enemies' is an injunction to behave
as if there are no enemies, since those we love can no longer be
described as enemies. The outward meaning is plain and it has the
most startling social consequences. The inner meaning is no less
startling, for it is the command to allow no forces operating within
our total personality to become regarded by the ego as 'threats'.
Do not cast away the shadow. Do not reject the anima. Do not
resist the promptings of the Self. For we know that, both outwardly
and inwardly, '. . . every city or house divided against itself shall
not stand' (Matt. 12.25). But it is not by *striving* that we keep

ourselves from falling; it is by the grace of God, by submission to the integrating influence of the Self.

I wrote of Jung's distinction between those who become conscious of the process of individuation working within them and the great majority of people who have no such awareness but in whom the process is working just the same. These two types can be compared with William James' 'twice born' and 'once born' believers. For the twice born, the spiritual life is a series of Damascus road experiences and the individual is highly conscious of his spiritual temper. For the once born, the life of faith is something taken for granted as a man takes for granted the fact that the pavement will bear his weight. He does not need to reflect on this, and the pavement supports him just the same. So there is no value in supposing that the man who seems to be unreflecting spiritually is any the less holy, saved or integrated than the man who enjoys thinking and talking about his religion, reading spiritual books and so on. Indeed, we have already noticed that to become preoccupied with one's spiritual state is an unhealthy disposition.

There is something almost careless about Christianity, something that bids us let go of anxiety, even or especially anxiety about religious matters: 'Wherefore, if God so clothe the grass of the field, which today, is, and tomorrow is cast into the oven, shall he not much more clothe you, O ye of little faith?' (Matt. 6.30). The man who is forever worrying about the state of his soul is a man divided; for anxiety about his own soul and the precise development of his spiritual life actually deflects his attention from God. And the anxiety itself impedes his progress. The advice of the Sermon on the Mount is rather to ' . . . seek ye first the kingdom of God' (Matt. 6.33). Similarly, the man who spends all his time fretting over whether the different aspects of his psyche are all in the right balance, thereby demonstrates that they are not in balance. A certain forgetfulness needs to be cultivated. This is forgetfulness combined with singlemindedness. We are to seek the kingdom of God. This means that our goal is to allow our will to be conformed to God's will. It means the realization that the Self is the origin and purpose of the personality and that it inhabits a deeper level than that of the chattering ego. 'Blessed are the pure in heart' (Matt. 5.8). As Kierkegaard says, to be pure in heart means to will one thing. That 'one thing' is the will of God, the purposes of the true Self. This is the antidote to all morbid pondering over whether I am saved or not – which usually amounts to whether I *feel* saved or not; for while we are to become forgetful in one sense, we are to become the very opposite of forgetful in the case of others. We shall fail continually, of course, but we should not be discouraged; our salvation does not after all depend upon our success. 'Love one another with a pure heart' (I Peter 1.22). 'This is my commandment, That ye love one another, as I have loved you' (John 15.12). 'For this is the message that ye heard from the beginning, that we should love one another' (I John 3.11). 'If we love one another, God dwelleth in us' (I John 4.12). What is this love and what does it involve?

It is the same love as that spoken of in the Old Testament where it says, 'Thou shalt love thy neighbour as thyself' (Lev. 19.18). The New Testament emphasizes that this is the only law (Matt. 19.19; 22.39; Mark 12.31). And we know that to love God is to love our true Self. Therefore, the similarities between Self-love and the love of our neighbour are not trivial; if we love our neighbour as ourself it means that we work for his salvation in the same way that the forces of our psyche work for our own salvation. And so loving God and loving our neighbour are, as it were, the 'outside' and the 'inside' of the same love. And the commandment, 'Therefore all things whatsoever ye would that men should do to you, do ye even so to them' is not simply a moral ideal but a piece of practical advice. The social world of individuals in all their many relationships is a replica of the inner, spiritual world of the soul. So what we would do for our own soul (our true Self) we do also for others.

We are meant to be to others as the archetypal figures of the psyche are to ourselves. This is the way in which we help bring about the integration of others. This is what is meant by loving our neighbour. In our everyday experience we find that another's inward spiritual life is projected out on to us. We should not resent this, but instead respect it and learn how to respond. This is very difficult to accomplish when someone projects his Shadow on to us and we begin to feel that we are the object of that person's hatred. We should try to recognize what is going on in these cases; we are not the real object of his malice but a convenient outward correspondence of the other person's Shadow. What then should we do? The New Testament tells us by reminding us of what Jesus did in the same circumstances: 'who, when he was reviled, reviled

not again' (I Peter 2.23). If we do revile those who revile us, then
we only give them gounds for their hatred, and since that makes
them feel justified, they then have no cause or encouragement to
look inward and discover the true spiritual significance of their
act. If we attack those who attack us, then the war has begun; if
we refuse to treat anyone as an enemy – love your enemies – then
conflict is dispelled. If we allow others to project this dark side on
to us and if we do not complain, then there is every reason to hope
that eventually they will come to see the inappropriateness of the
projection and that they will begin to glimpse their Shadow. That
is the start of spiritual development. Of course, it is hard for us to
do this because we do not like to be blamed for what we have not
done; we find it difficult to absorb the darkness that is cast upon
us. Nevertheless, the way is pointed out quite clearly: 'Bear ye one
another's burdens, and so fulfil the law of Christ.'

A practical consequence of acting in this way is measured by
the extent to which the other person, having encountered his own
Shadow at least partly due to my refusal to 'become' his faulty
nature, finds himself able to trust me as a friend. This is the true
function of a friend – to be an aid and comfort to the other while
he is discovering his own dark side. For it is important that at this
time of bewilderment and self-disgust, he has someone on hand
who, though having been made very aware of the other's faults,
still values him and offers affection. This is also why really close
friendships are vulnerable: in casual acquaintance I hide my
Shadow beneath politeness and social ritual but my friend sees
through all outward show to the darkness which exists in my soul;
it is this darkness also that he is called upon to bear and sometimes
the strain becomes too great. So, in the story from Genesis, Cain
kills his brother Abel; but it is the Christian's duty to give his
brother life. The one who sticks to his friend warts and all, through
thick and thin, is the good friend; it is he who helps his friend come
to terms with his own dark side. My friend remains my friend not
because of my dark side but because he can see another side to my
personality – the side which is in danger of being overwhelmed by
the presence of the Shadow. And because he remains my friend, I
am less likely to be overwhelmed by my own self-disgust. There
are many examples in the New Testament in which one character
is unable to accept his brother's dark side. Consider the parable

of the Prodigal Son and in particular the elder son's words to his
father:

> Lo, these many years do I serve thee, neither transgressed I at
> any time thy commandment: and yet thou never gavest me a
> kid, that I might make merry with my friends: but as soon as
> this thy son was come, which hath devoured thy living with
> harlots, thou has killed for him the fatted calf (Luke 15.29–30).

The psychologist detects projection on a grand scale here, as the
elder son's words show that with his own dark side he wishes he
had done the same as his younger brother! We can hardly doubt
that, were the father not standing between them, the two brothers
would soon be involved in a brawl with each other. Moral chaos
is loosed because their Shadows are out of control. Resentment
and attempts at self-justification are emotions and deeds which
come to us more readily than acts of acceptance and forgiveness –
especially if, like the elder son, we make the mistake of actually
believing that we are justified! For we see what happens to him:
as soon as he protests his own case he loses it by that very
protestation. 'As it is written, there is none righteous, no, not one'
(Rom. 3 10).

But there is another aspect of the Shadow's work which we are
called upon to perform for our neighbour and that is the work of
criticism. I do not mean carping for the sake of carping – for that
can soon become merely a projection of my own Shadow. I mean
the task which Satan performed when he met Christ in the story
of the temptations in the wilderness. He voiced the alternative and
by so doing he forced Christ to question his own motives and
thereby to deepen the understanding of his vocation. We have
already seen how it is a naïve spirituality which regards the
character of Satan as something which is to be shunned. Of course,
his suggestions are ultimately rejected, but the character of Satan
is as necessary to the story told by the Gospel writers as the
character of Jesus himself. We know that, in the inner life, the
person of Satan is the Shadow; in the everyday life of the world,
men and women are obliged to play his rôle. And, as in so much
else connected with the spiritual life, that rôle is better played by
those who are aware of the fact that they are playing it. That it is
played, even by those who have no understanding of what they are

doing, is demonstrated by every playground squabble and saloon bar brawl.

Real friendship is far removed from mere niceness, from a polite acceptance of everything that the other does; it is the antithesis of all that cosiness and pop-ecclesiastical *bonhommie* which is to be found in the congregations of the fashionably religious where criticism is dismissed as 'negative'. True criticism is creative, else why was Jesus led by *the Spirit* into the wilderness? True criticism also demonstrates the closeness of our relationship with our neighbour, for it is only when I really understand and identify with his hopes and fears that I am able to make pertinent and constructive criticisms. The critic enables the one he is criticizing to make subtle and important alterations in his direction. The creative artist knows this perhaps better than anyone else, and he cries out for informed and argued criticism so that he may redirect and improve his work. To reject criticism is not to disapprove of 'negativity'; it is to make an idol of arrogance, to suppose that one's own position is unassailable.

Criticism provided by the friend in the guise of the shadow may be of ideas and schemes of course, but it is also often more direct and personal than that. You remember the advertisement about 'body odour'? 'Even his best friend would not tell him'. So it is my job to draw attention to my friend's harmful characteristics, to those which I as outsider can see while to him they remain invisible, and which impede his spiritual development. And, if possible, I should do this without glee or rancour, without that dark joy *(Schadenfreude)* which seems to take a delight in the shortcomings of others, without, that is, projecting my own Shadow on to my friend. It is better to have insight into one's actions than not to have it; but it remains true that, even in the practice of Shadenfreude, some good is accomplished. For, whether the critic's motives are entirely pure or not, the actual criticism which he makes is the most important thing.

Jesus often criticized his disciples, sometimes in strong language. In the story of the walk to Emmaus he said, 'O fools, and slow of heart to believe all that the prophets have spoken' (Luke 24.25). And this is after the saying 'whosoever shall say, Thou fool, shall be in danger of hell fire' (Matt. 5.22)! He also said to Peter, 'Get thee behind me Satan' (Matt. 16.23). And to all the disciples, 'O ye of little faith' (Matt. 6.30). These critical remarks are besides all the violent denunciations of the Pharisees. We might conjecture that the disciples' acceptance of Jesus' criticisms and the Pharisees' rejection of the criticisms levelled at them reflects the existence and non-existence of *Schadenfreude* (Jesus projecting his own Shadow) in the incidents respectively. His criticisms of the disciples reveal the intention to inform and to correct while those of the Pharisees are outright condemnations. Might we further conjecture that Jesus would have had more success with the Pharisees if he had tried to sympathize with their position a little more? Here we are up against the problem of whether one should be tolerant of intolerance. In my opinion, Jesus displayed the only attitude which it is possible to display towards smug self-righteousness; for it is only the self-righteous who are impervious to the gospel of forgiveness precisely because they do not think that they are in any need of it. 'For I am not come to call the righteous, but sinners to repentance' (Matt. 9.13) says Jesus with more than a touch of irony. The Pharisees whom he addresses are those who 'trusted that they were righteous and despised others' (Luke 18.9). There is no one beyond the reach of the gospel, no one who is unable to make progress towards that integration of the personality which the New Testament calls 'the Kingdom of Heaven' except the one who will have nothing to do with it, the one who cannot confess because he sees nothing to confess, who cannot accommodate his Shadow because he does not acknowledge its existence. This is the meaning of those disturbing words: 'All manner of sin and blasphemy shall be forgiven unto men but the blasphemy against the Holy Ghost shall not be forgiven unto men' (Matt. 12.31). This should not be seen as a spiteful judgment on the part of capricious omniscience, but as a deep spiritual and psychological truth: that which is not confessed can never be forgiven; and only *because* it is not confessed can it not be forgiven. How can anyone begin to rethink, to redirect himself, when he thinks he is going in the right direction already?

So, in terms of analytical psychology, Christian ethics commands us to allow others to project their Shadows on to us. This enables my neighbour to become aware of his own dark side, whereas, if I were to resist and complain about his behaviour, he would be diverted towards my irritation and away from his own Shadow. If my neighbour is to be saved, he must begin by acknowledging his own dark side just as I must. Since my neighbour's salvation (his psychological and spiritual health) is my concern, I must do all that I can to enable him to perceive his

Shadow. I must do nothing to hinder him. This is the meaning of Matthew 5.39, 'But I say unto you that ye resist not evil: but whosoever shall smite thee on thy right cheek, turn to him the other also.' This dramatic verse sums up all that is involved in my attitude towards my brother's dark side. It is a short but complete parable which exactly explains what a Christian's attitude should be towards *another's* evil. By striking my attacker in return for his blows, I shall succeed only in prolonging the fight with the result that the original violence will seem justified by my retaliation. Turning the other cheek is the means by which I give the attacker two clear opportunities to identify the real nature of his aggression. Returning good for evil in this way was recommended long before the teaching of Jesus: 'if thine enemy be hungry, give him bread to eat; and if he be thirsty, give him water to drink' (Prov. 25.21). But the motive for this behaviour could not be described as Christian. The next verse says, 'For thou shalt heap coals of fire on his head'. When Paul quotes this verse, he is careful to put it within the context of the gospel. He adds, 'Be not overcome of evil, but overcome evil with good' (Rom. 12.21).

Moralizers and preachers of respectability do not find them-selves the victims of crucifixion. Whatever the final reason for Jesus' execution, we may assume that at least part of the accusation against him was prompted by the sheer outrageousness of his teaching. Here is the teacher who despises the moralizing of the established teachers. St Mark says he is not like them; he teaches 'with authority and not as the scribes' (1.22). He pardons the adulterer. He claims that the sinner is rather justified than the man who thinks himself righteous. He locates virtue in meekness and gentleness among those who are poor in spirit – or simply 'poor' (Luke 6.20). Above all he teaches the forgiveness of sins and love for the enemy. This sort of teaching is truly subversive because it overturns all the accepted conventions of social life which is in effect a system of allowances and prohibitions, of rewards and punishments and of justification by works. The scribes and Phar-isees of all ages are, by contrast with Jesus, like Nietzsche's 'Hypocrites'; they 'say they desire morality when all they really desire is the police'. And many have been those who would call themselves Christians but who in the event have behaved more like the scribes. Nowhere is this more true than in the case of sexual ethics.

3 | Sex and Sanctification

The hypocrite introduces his concept of sexual ethics only where there is a question of physical contact. But this is not what Jesus says at all. 'But I say unto you, That whosoever looketh on a woman to lust after her hath committed adultery with her already in his heart' (Matt. 5. 28). In practice people do not believe this; instead they make lust into a crime which is defined in terms of touching. And so long as they themselves do not touch, they feel qualified to stand in judgment over those who do. So the adulterer is condemned by the church founded upon the teaching of Jesus, whereas Jesus himself did the opposite and forgave. Even the divorcée is disapproved of and in some places disallowed the sacraments. It is unimaginable that Jesus would have regarded 'sexual sinners' in this way; indeed we have the clearest evidence that he did not so regard them. I do not believe that Jesus said all those things about divorce to be found in Matthew 5.31–32. And this opinion is not based on the unfair principle of partisan selection of texts; it is based on a reliable principle of literary criticism which excludes from authentic authorship anything that is plainly out of character with the main body of the work. If Jesus really did say those legalistic words about divorce, then it is hard to see him as the same man who gave us the rest of that Sermon on the Mount.

By making lust in the heart the criterion of adultery, Jesus is simply saying that we are all guilty – if 'guilty' is the right word. For we can hardly avoid 'guilt' of this sort, since we are biologically arranged and constructed to desire sexual relationships. And it is not possible to command feelings of this or any other sort, for while a commandment is a linguistic and therefore a rational thing, a feeling is non-rational. Only what is rational can be made the subject of commandment or of instruction of any kind. Puritan attempts to quell the biological urge by all means – including cold baths, healthy exercise and clothing women in the dowdiest fashions – are consequently misguided. Jesus knew that we all feel sexual desire and his saying about adultery in the heart is a reminder to hypocrites that they are not exempt. Since we are all guilty, it ill becomes us to condemn anyone who happens to be more 'obviously' guilty than the rest.

The hypocrite's outrage at sexual sins is a projection of his own sexual guilt and frustration. The mechanics of this projection and the reasons for it have been well enough described by Freud, and his conclusions do not contradict but serve to enlarge upon the spiritual understanding of the Gospels. Projection of this sort is a common human failing and it is frequently aired in fiction. Anyone who has read Somerset Maugham's short story *Rain* will appreciate how deadly this projection can be, how destructive of genuine relationships and how damaging to the process of personal development and the integration of the personality.

The anima-animus syzygy of analytical psychology provides us with a good guide as to how we might more constructively understand sexual relationships. In an earlier chapter we discussed the appearance and internal, psychological development of the anima as one part of the whole individual. We also saw how the phases of the anima within are matched by characters in the external worlds of every day life and imaginative fiction. The personification of the anima as child, virgin, temptress, helper, wisdom and virtue provides an external correspondence – an objective correlative – for the various stages of inner, psychological development. If we turn this psychology, this spirituality, the other way about, we see it as ethics. And this we are bound to do once we see that, in fact, the personifications are real; they are the people we meet in daily life. The task for Christian morality is to help others achieve the same sort of integration and fulfilment as we desire for ourselves. Thus spirituality and ethics are inseparable. They are the inside and the outside of the same thing. This is the psychological meaning of the text, 'Ye shall know them by their fruits' (Matt. 7.16). For a man's practical morality is the outward image of his inner life. It is not a case of one thing *causing* the other, but of two aspects of one and the same thing.

It follows that, just as in our spiritual lives we should do nothing to hinder proper progress, we are responsible for the progress of others. For as they are images of our inner spiritual workings, so we are images of theirs. And so it is logically impossible for us to do anything about our own psychological development without involving others. It is not a question of our relationships with God *obliging* us to be nice to others – as if ethics were an awful forfeit which we have to pay for our spirituality. It is rather that our relationship with God (or the Self) is but another aspect of our relationship with others. 'Love thy neighbour as thyself' (Lev. 18.18). And it is this psychological understanding which John is trying to teach when he writes, 'If a man say, I love God, and hateth his brother, he is a liar: for he that loveth not his brother whom he hath seen, how can he love God whom he hath not seen?' The word 'can' in that verse has logical as well as moral force. It is both true and frightening to realize that our moral conduct is an image of our spirituality; and the condition of my soul is best discovered by an examination of how I deal with my neighbour.

The intimate connection between character and behaviour, between spirituality and ethics, has even more revealing consequences for the understanding of morality. For example, it demonstrates that the moralizer, the legalistic preacher of righteousness, is bound in his own soul by the proscriptions of law; otherwise he would not act in the way that he does. Only the man whose own inner life is governed by grace can go beyond legalism in his outward behaviour and live the life of the gospel, the central characteristic of which is forgiveness. And the preacher who makes his gospel a matter of legislation and commandments *by so doing* reveals that he himself is not governed by grace how ever frequently he might use that word. 'Can the blind lead the blind? Shall they not both fall into the ditch?' (Luke 6.39).

Christian morality is the life of grace between man and his neighbour. Just as grace is the means of individual justification and sanctification, so it is the principle upon which our relationships with others should be based. Indeed we must go further and say that sanctification and psychological wholeness are based not only on the individual's inner experience, the turmoil of his own religious quest, but upon the way he lives in society. 'The kingdom of God is within you' is also translated 'The kingdom of God is among you' (Luke 17.21). Salvation is between man and God, but it is also between man and man. And the one is not a consequence or a cause of the other, but both are aspects of the one process. Since the whole of salvation, individual and social, is founded upon grace, it follows that no one has the right to adopt a legalistic or judgmental attitude towards his neighbour. 'Judge not, that ye be not judged' (Matt. 7.1). This becomes crucial once we realize that man judged is man condemned, for judgment is always according to law and all men have always fallen short of the perfect righteousness which the law demands.

So if our own goal is sanctification, if we desire peace of soul or psychological wholeness, we must will from the bottom of our hearts the sanctification of our neighbour. Of course, it is not a question of our being commanded to do this, as if we could achieve love for our neighbour by striving; it is a case first of all of believing that salvation is by grace and not by law and then by allowing grace to begin to operate in our lives. There is more passivity, at least in the beginning, than activity about this. And it is closely associated with prayer and meditation, an opening of the heart, a willingness to 'let-be'. As we progress, we come to realize that the test of our sanctification is not ecstatic experience or spiritual exaltation, but that it is to be detected in the ordinary associations of every day. The New Testament is explicit: 'We know that we have passed from death to life, *because we love* the brethren' (I John 3.14). Existentialist philosophers were fond of saying 'Hell is other people'. In Christian ethics, by contrast, the only way to heaven is by other people. If we may borrow an existentialist insight, it is true to say that other people are the raw material for the development of our personality; but any temptation to impersonality, to objectify others in the way that makes them purely for our benefit, is swiftly dispelled by the realization that we exist for the same benefit of others.

We have seen how this begins to work out in practice in the case of the Shadow and of how that particular aspect receives social as well as individual application in both our willingness to bear without resentment the dark projections of others and also our function as questioners and prompters of our neighbour's attitudes. We are called upon to play something of Satan's rôle, not in any macabre or malevolent sense but in his wilderness capacity.

Without the person of Satan, that projection of his own dark side, Christ at the beginning of his ministry would never have been able to decide upon his next moves. That personification of the dark aspects is nothing more than the process of discernment, the evaluation of alternatives. By receiving the dark projections of others and by acting occasionally as questioners and prompters, we enable them similarly to evaluate and to discern, to discover something of their own nature – a prerequisite for any subsequent spiritual development. The long journey towards perfection can only begin with the acknowledgment of our imperfection – 'If we say we have no sin, we deceive ourselves and the truth is not in us' (I John 1.8) – and for that acknowledgment we require the graceful complicity of others.

The ego's relationship with the anima is paralleled in social life by relationships between the sexes. A man will repeatedly find real women, or images of real women, who will outwardly personify events which are taking place inwardly in his psychological development. A similar process takes place in a woman's development. It is not a case of either sex being dominant or superior, but of reciprocity. In the working out of personal and sexual relationships of this type, it is of great value to understand the inner, spiritual aspects as well as the objective and observable liaison. A young woman may not understand why the young man finds her to be so fascinating and alluring that he becomes tongue-tied every time they meet; but in the maturing relationship, she will learn not only the answer to that puzzle but also much about herself. In a love affair, the man unconsciously projects his anima (his soul) on to the objective woman; and so by the light of the image then projected, he comes to learn more about his own inner life. Marriage is thus rightly called both a vocation and a sacrament because it is one of the archetypal paths to sanctification and, as something which is (like the wedding ring) 'given and received', it is a means of grace. The partners discover in each other aspects of their own selves which otherwise might have lain hidden forever.

This is also the psychological justification of monogamy for it is only through an ordered relationship over many years that worthwhile understanding and progressive enlightenment can be achieved. Promiscuity or so-called 'serial monogamy' is a sign that self-knowledge is lacking. A man goes from one woman to another because he does not know the nature of his own unconscious. He thinks he sees it perhaps as he falls madly in love; but soon it is lost or else it has suffered abrupt dissociation as he tires of the first woman and looks for another. It is impossible for genuine progress to be made in this way. The liturgist who advocated marriage in the words 'mutual society, help and comfort' *(Book of Common Prayer)* knew that these things are not accomplished in weeks.

The order and structure of sexual relationships should follow the order and structure of the inner life, or else there is only neurosis and dissociation with all the uncertainty and distress which they bring. A brief relationship is almost bound to be of a trivial kind. The process of getting to know another person – like that of discovering one's own spiritual identity – is a life-long task. The hedonism of all ages recoils from this task, from this responsibility, by taking refuge in the excitement and glamour which are often to be found in brief encounters. And it takes no account of the psychological reasons for monogamy, dismissing them as 'old fashioned prudishness' or 'mere moralizing'. Whereas, the truth is that a man who is not prepared to work at a lifelong relationship with another person is very likely to be the same man who will not give the right sort of attention to his own spiritual development. Of course, marriage is not the only vocation; but it is interesting to note that the alternatives to marriage – celibacy, certain religious orders and so on – usually involve the same sorts of vows and commitments required in marriage itself.

In my work as a parish priest, I have many couples who began by thinking that extramarital relationships both could and should be accepted as part of a natural, reasonable and thoroughly modern mode of procedure. 'We thought we had got rid of all those old taboos', said one parishioner. But I have not come across a single case where these relationships are enjoined, by one partner or by both, where the marriage has escaped crisis. I do not say that every marriage has ended on the rocks; in some there has been forgiveness and reconciliation. But, because sexual relationships are the outward aspect of profound and powerful inner developments, it is extremely unlikely (and perhaps even impossible) that they can be regarded as trivial. Casual sex is anything but casual.

It is easy to see why monogamy is so unpopular; it can be very tedious. But the process of self-understanding is also tedious at times. Falling in love is, as it were, the social event which parallels the individual event of baptism, conversion or initiation. It is a zenith surrounded and infused by numinous power and magical symbolism. But after the peak of initiation there is the valley of pilgrimage. We might almost say that after the baptism comes the temptation!

The marriage, like the individual, must encounter its own Shadow, its own dark side. This may show itself as boredom, as finding one another's behaviour and mannerisms annoying, as feeling that the magic has gone out of the relationship. But it has not gone out. It can never go out. Where, after all would it go? It is always there, but it needs to be consistently rediscovered. Each rediscovery will be stronger than the ones preceding in just the same way that there is an intensification of glory in the Zenith symbolism of the life of Christ from baptism to transfiguration, to resurrection and ascension. But the gain in strength is a result of the mundane and painful events in between – the wilderness, doubts, fears insecurity, persecutions. There are demons on the way as well, one of which might be characterized adultery. Just as, symbolically, the demons are cast out, so the act of adultery can be forgiven and the relationship restored. I cannot see why there was so much fuss when the Bishop of Winchester said that adultery was not unforgivable – unless of course this derives from the projected lust of 'respectable' Chiristians! The gospel is that *all* confessed sins are forgivable; if not, where is the good news? The Old Testament book of Hosea likens the relationship between God and Israel to that between a husband and an unfaithful wife. The final forgiveness and reconciliation in the last chapter of Hosea amounts to a certainty that relationships can be renewed and restored even after the most hurtful unfaithfulness. And there is another way of looking at this parable about God and the chosen people: it is to see human relationships as images of God and his love for his people; and to appreciate the great value which the prophet ascribes to these human relationships by speaking of God in the same terms. As adultery is to marriage so is idolatry to faith.

A sacrament is always a unifying gift. So the Bible describes the man and his wife as 'one flesh' (Gen. 2.24). In psychological terms this means that each finds completeness in the other; and they find this in a way that is the hallmark of Christianity – grace and self-giving. The relationship between a man and a woman deepens as each gives to the other. This is exactly what we have come to expect in the paradoxical scheme of Christian doctrine: we are made full as we empty ourselves.

Not everyone marries of course. Not everyone is able to marry. What then is the social aspect of their salvation? Where do they discover reciprocity if it is not in a marriage? I think it is true to say that the unmarried receive this only partially. This is not to suggest that there is something morally inferior about the single person or the homosexual; only that common experience shows marriage to be a natural corollary of individual psychological development as well as one of society's principle institutions. At the very least, therefore, psychological development for the unmarried is bound to be more difficult than it is for the married – as the arduousness of the monastic discipline shows. For the married person there are many more naturally available outward correlations of his inner development than are found in the single life. The single person simply has less help. Of course, progress is possible in whatever state a man finds himself but, by every criterion – social, historical, scriptural, statistical and so on – marriage is the norm. That is why other kinds of lasting relationships, as for example between homosexuals, tend to replicate marriage as closely as possible. Once more I would stress that no culpability is affirmed of these 'alternatives'; a good homosexual relationship – one in which there is faithfulness and trust, love and self-sacrifice – is much to be preferred to a bad marriage consumed by wrath, strife and jealousy. But I still believe that the homosexual needs more personal strength than the married man in order to continue and to improve his relationship; for it is the homosexual who is the outsider and who incurs the odium of society. His ostracism is not of his own doing but it is a result of the very existence of marriage as a social and psychological norm. As such it is understandable, since man is constituted of emotions as well as rationality and therefore his most important institutions and customs are bound to possess something of the nature of the taboo.

But the man with insight into the supra-rational nature of his and his society's make-up will not condemn the outsider, the one who deviates from the norm; he will rather do all he can to favour and help him, as Jesus did for the outcasts of his own day. It is hard to avoid the criticism that one is merely stigmatizing all who do not conform to the norm as either immoral or sick. But there is in the very nature and definition of all forms of non-conformity something of incompleteness, of deficit. This is necessarily true because the one who puts himself (or is put by others) outside the conventions of society cannot, by definition, then avail himself of the full benefits which those conventions have to offer. The outsider lives outside. Nor do I wish to deny the existence of other benefits which the outsider may possess – benefits not normally available to the conformist. Some of these are, in fact, well-known: they include the usual signs and 'privileges' of belonging to a sub-culture, such as comradeship, a sense of special identity and a more acute sense of belonging – since those with whom one belongs are fewer in number than the main social group. If they can also include aggressiveness, paranoia and exclusivism, well, that is but one more illustration of the fact that every phenomenon has its dark side.

The duty of the insider is to the outsider, to help and support him, to be compassionate without being patronizing and above all not to judge him. For however strong the normal conventions, however certain are the usual pathways, they chiefly show their strength and self-confidence in toleration of the dissident. Sexual persecution, like religious persecution, has its origin in the unconscious doubts of its practitioners.

Just as, in New Testament times the leper faced the daily prospect of starvation as a social consequence of his condition, so today's sexual outsider is vulnerable to the assaults of depravity. The man who cannot find his fulfilment in marriage, for whatever reason, is much more likely to turn to pornography and to other expressions of sexuality which are destructive. This fact reflects the awful moral karma which Jesus spoke of in the words: 'For whosoever hath, to him shall be given, and he shall have more abundance: but whosoever hath not, from him shall be taken away even that he hath' (Matt. 13.12). Once again the burden of responsibility for such outsiders is upon the Christian who must not simply legislate or condemn as the Pharisees legislated and condemned in their day. The one who knows anything of the gospel will rather be compassionate – but his compassion will be more than a moral imperative deduced from his faith; it will be a natural consequence of the ripening wholeness of his being. For compassion that is only commanded is not compassion. The law has no power to save. 'For in Christ Jesus neither circumcision availeth any thing, nor uncircumcision, but a new creature' (Gal. 6.15). That new creature is the gift of grace working within us for sanctification; the power of the unconscious forces, when accommodated by co-operating consciousness, to bring about wholeness. So it becomes clear that the one who persists in legislating and condemning knows nothing of Christ. He may know the law, of course; but that is a different matter.

4 | Society

In Christian morality, as in any other ethical system, it is not possible to draw a clear division between individual and social aspects. My duty usually means my duty to others. Christianity goes further in that it insists upon love of the brethren as the very mark and definition of faith. It is not the case that Christians love one another as a result of certain beliefs which they hold; it is rather that their love for one another is exactly what is meant by their Christianity.

So when the Christian, like everyone else, is forced to face the issues of contemporary social ethics, his response will be in terms of this love. And love is nothing other than the gift conferred by grace which enables the recipient to desire the wholeness of others as he desires his own personal wholeness. Indeed, the two desires are one and the same. In psychological terms, the growth of psychic integration both shows me that this is 'the good' for every man and it enables me to will that good wholeheartedly. In the case just mentioned, that of pornography, I should not merely avoid its degradation myself, but I should do all I can to help others avoid it. As the authors of *The Williams Report* wrote, 'Pornography is trash, ugly and shallow'. It is my Christian duty so to fill the life and experience of my neighbour with true value that he is not subject to that which is degrading. There is a warning here not just for those involved in the production of what is generally termed pornography, but for all who lay before the public forms of information and entertainment. Much of the shallow trash that appears on television under the description 'light entertainment' is not harmless diversion but a process by which the public is belittled and demeaned. Those who put on such programmes are saying, in fact, 'There: find your notion of what is humorous or enjoyable in *that!*'. 'Or what man is there of you, whom if his son ask for bread, will he give him a stone?' (Matt. 7.9). Of course, if he has never tasted bread but lived only on what he could lick from the underside of stones, he will not recognize bread when he tastes it for the first time; he might not even like it. He may have to learn to like it.

There is a parallel between the education of the palate and the long, slow process of inner, psychological and spiritual development. Merely to rage at the pornographer and to be disgusted by the person addicted to it is to spit in the teeth of the wind. It is the Christian's task to provide things of true quality and to be himself a sign of wholeness so that all that is unwholesome and spiritually destructive can be seen for what it is. To ban pornography (even if this could be done) and to offer no alternative amounts to a rejection of the person who is captivated by it. I am not talking only about so called 'dirty pictures' but what are we to say of the soul of the youngster who goes around all day listening to trashy music through 'personalized headphones'? What are we to say of the institution that provides such drivel on constant tap? Perhaps we shall say the same as we say of the society which condemns so many industrial workers to similar acts of mindless repetition in the factories. And it is no use arguing that, while in the case of the factories there is no choice, there is a choice in the case of the music. For choice itself must be educated and education as a part of spiritual development is slow. There are questions here also for those who provide cheap music as the staple diet in liturgy.

And then there are the other contentions of social ethics where life and death, the good of the individual weighed against the good of society are involved. What is the Christian's attitude towards the death penalty for condemned murderers? I do not believe that the Christian conscience allows such a punishment, for death is to deny the possibility of repentance and recreation, reconstruction of the personality. It is also the most extreme act of projection. It is my Shadow I am trying to kill when I approve the death sentence for murder. The gospel is quite clear:

Ye have heard that is was said by them of old time, Thou shalt not kill; and whosoever shall kill shall be in danger of the judgment: But I say unto you, that whosoever is angry with his brother without a cause shall be in danger of the judgment . . . (Matt. 5.22–23).

In my heart I am as guilty as any murderer. Christian ethics consists in really believing this to be true; it does not consist in the mere repetition of the saying out of vapid piety. At the same time, sentimentality and the flaws of naïve understanding have no part in morality. If the gospel is about the wholeness of the murderer it is also about the wholeness of his potential victims. I have the right, and I may even have the duty, to lay down my own life, but I do not have the right to sacrifice the lives of others. Thus the murderer must be restrained while he is being helped. The same is true in the case of all criminals. Because we are a whole society and not just a collection of isolated individuals, some sort of Christian utilitarianism is necessary – one in which 'the greatest happiness' is described in terms of salvation or psychological integration. If we take seriously those verses from Matthew, if we really believe that none of us is free from the dissociation and incompleteness that the Bible calls 'sin', then we shall realize that to kill another, even by judicious process, is to compound the original act of murder: for just as the first victim's psychological development was ended by his murder, so that of the murderer is ended by our judgment. A gospel that insists on the good of my neighbour could never countenance such an act.

Psychologically, I have also compounded my own dissociation if I consent to the murderer's death, because this consent involves me in an extreme projection of my own Shadow. So long as I detect greater evil in others, I shall not detect it in myself. This is why the effect on the judge, the courts and the hangman, and upon a whole society which sanctions capital punishment, must be taken into consideration. The so called 'effect on the punishers' is not an empty phrase; it is an unavoidable psychological consequence of the act of taking life. If every man's death diminishes me, then that death which I most directly cause diminishes me the most.

Another case in which I might be asked to end the life of another is that of euthanasia. Is this any different from murder? If murder is defined as wrongful killing, is there a sort of killing which is, or in certain circumstances might be, right? If we are to judge by our main criterion which is that everything should be done to help and encourage others towards spiritual wholeness, then the answer might appear simple: euthanasia cannot be right because it ends life, and life itself is the first prerequisite for spiritual growth. Some do indeed hold this view which they support by powerful arguments drawn from past experiences of individuals who have endured the most appalling suffering and yet who have persevered in the faith and even found their faith strengthened through their suffering. But these are not the only experiences. Men and women, so far from achieving serenity in a terminal illness, sometimes die in a state of awful physical and spiritual torture. I believe that there can be no clear and absolute ruling in this matter. However, since it is not what happens to us that is crucial for our spiritual progress but how we accommodate what happens to us, the ideal must involve the acceptance and transformation of suffering even up to death. Christian utilitarianism defines 'happiness' in 'the greatest happiness of the greatest number' not as some sort of trivial satisfaction or even as the avoidance of pain; rather the definition will be in terms of spiritual wholeness. And, as we know, progress towards wholeness can take place during extreme suffering and it can even be helped by suffering. So the Christian will not be quick to switch off the life-support equipment.

But there are cases in which it would be cruel and mistaken to prolong life. For instance, there is the case of the person injured in a road accident so severely that, according to all the most reliable indicators of medical technology and ordinary commonsense, he has no consciousness at all, and no likelihood of regaining consciousness. I am thinking of incidences of severe head injuries but where there has been little or no damage to the rest of the body, so that heart, lungs and all the other organs are working normally. The sort of life which then remains is, as far as we can tell, only residual. And to claim that 'as far as we can tell' may not be the whole truth and that therefore the injured person's life should be prolonged as long as possible because he might still be spiritually alive and developing on some plane of which we have no understanding is a superstitious argument. For we must always act on our best information. (What would it mean in terms of consequences if we were to act on less than our best information?) If, as far as we can tell, there is no mental life left in the patient, then we must conclude that there is no mental life left. Otherwise we no longer know what we mean by 'mental life'. Besides if it is argued that spiritual life might continue even when the brain is catastrophically injured, then we must conclude that this would be a spiritual life which did not *depend* upon the health of the brain. By pulling the plug on the life-support system I destroy only the brain; medical technology, however advanced, has no influence over concepts of non-mental spiritual life.

There are less extreme cases, however, in which the decision is by no means as easy. Imagine a woman of seventy-nine who is dying of cancer. She is in what the best medical opinion regards as the last few days of her life. She still suffers pain though she is heavily drugged. Moreover, she is horrified by what is happening to her. Further imagine that she has always let it be known within her family – and she has put it in writing – that, if ever she were to find herself in the state just described, the family acting with the doctors should over-dose her so that she would pass peacefully and without pointless delay from her sufferings. I believe that, in such a case, it is the duty of the family and of the doctors to carry out the patient's wishes. It is true that, even in such extremity, some human beings continue to make spiritual progress in the teeth of their sufferings; but this is by no means always true, and it is equally obvious that in many cases all talk of spiritual progress under the circumstances is out of place. These are difficult decisions, but the Christian must not expect to be exempted from such decisions.

The question about whether anyone should prescribe his own euthanasia cannot be avoided; it is, of course, the problem of suicide. I believe that, since further progress, revelation, enlightenment, self-acceptance and so on are always possible, it is wrong to end one's own life. But I know that this is an ideal solution and that, more often than not, particular circumstances are not much like any ideal. All principles need to be modified in terms of the principle of mercy. Usually, it is those who are most advanced spiritually who are able to face terminal suffering and, by their faith and experience, to transform it so that death becomes less terrifying for others who observe their example. Sometimes a painful illness brings greater awareness and understanding to one who has spent the most part of his earlier life quite oblivious of spiritual realities and his inner life. But in many other cases there is only terror and dread. Whatever the 'ideal', it can hardly be right for anyone, let alone the Christian, to prolong the life of such a sufferer; whether it is right or wrong for him to wish to prolong his own life in similar circumstances will finally depend on the quality of his own religious experience. In any case, while we rightly admire the saint who bears his tribulations serenely, it is no part of Christian ethics to condemn those who are unable to display such courage. For ourselves, we must hope that we might always use whatever evil comes the better to assist our spiritual progress; we might even begin to put that hope into practice already, before we are afflicted, and to try and understand the nature of our inner being and what things make for psychological wholeness. For whoever refuses the call to look inwards will find, when the outward parts fail, that he has no place wherein his true Self can be contained (Luke 12.20).

I am making no attempt to do more than sketch an outline of the sort of Christian ethics which might be inferred or deduced from the theological/psychological perspective of the earlier chapters. Those who found those chapters helpful might also find this outline of ethics to be something with which they are in broad agreement; but there will always be divergences on particular issues. It will be obvious by now that I am writing under the difficulty of wanting to deny all place to legalism but at the same time as seeing the necessity for describing ethics in terms of the very definite structure and limits of the psyche. The gospel urges us to avoid wrongdoing; but it insists we are not justified by this avoidance. We are justified only by faith which is a gift of grace. However, if we persist in wrongdoing – I do not mean disobedience to rules and laws invented by man but that disobedience which is the result of ignorance or carelessness of the nature of our psychological make-up – we shall not be able to avoid the consequences. I believe that this is a version of what Paul said in Romans when he insisted that the wrath of God falls on all wrongdoers whether they are inside the law or outside it (see especially Rom. 2 and 3). It is interesting to note what C. H. Dodd says in his commentary on Romans of this concept of wrath; he describes it as a power which does not have its origin in divine passion but which is the inevitable fate of those who go the wrong way.

My claim, throughout this book and particularly in this chapter, is that spiritual chaos is unavoidable where there is ignorance or carelessness of spiritual realities. This chaos, which might well be described as wrath, is not of God; it is rather the result of ignoring God. In psychological language, it is the dissociation of the personality which is bound to occur while ever a person fails to notice and to attend to the structure and development of his own psyche. Of course the man who constantly projects his Shadow, who tirelessly resists the promptings of the anima and the manifestation of the Self will finish up in chaos and wrath. How else should we expect him to finish up? I believe that, *from the psychological point of view – that is from the perspective of experience*, God and the Self may be regarded as one and the same thing. It is not a question of reductionism or of wanting to deny anything; it is purely a matter of choice of language. Traditional theology says that it is not God's fault if I sin; he does not cause my sin. The language of analytical psychology expresses the same thing by saying that it is not the archetype of the Self which causes psychological dissociation. Just as God is always ready to hear sinners and to forgive them, so the resources of the Self are always available to the ego in the progress towards the integration of the personality. And just as God requires repentance, so the resources of the Self cannot become available until the ego begins to look inwards. I do not even mean to suggest that these are the only two languages in which we may speak of spiritual/psychological realities; but that, because of changes in sensibility (and in the workings of language itself) brought about by the discoveries and techniques of our time, for some people the language of analytical psychology might mediate these realities with a directness no longer possessed by the old 'God language'. It is not the language, whichever one we choose, that is basic; but the unavoidable spiritual/psychological experiences which language attempts to describe. To make a god out of any particular language – that is to insist upon it to the exclusion of other ways of talking – is a recrudescence of the old sin of idolatry. And real atheism does not consist in the denial of a particular doctrine or image of a Supreme Being but in the refusal to admit that there is anything of value in spiritual or psychological experiences.

The thorough reductionist is not the man who rejects 'God language' or the language of analytical psychology; he is rather the one who believes that all such languages, including the ancient myths and stories which speak analogically of man's nature and place in the world, are worthless. This kind of reductionism not only ignores the experience of the past (of religious tradition and the idea of the collective unconscious) but also present experience. For no one can avoid for very long the inner workings of his own personality of which all the religious, mythological and psychological languages are pictures. That is the meaning of Psalm 139:

> Whither shall I go from thy spirit?
>   or whither shall I flee from thy presence?
> If I ascend up into heaven, thou art there:
>   if I make my bed in hell, behold thou art there:
> If I take the wings of the morning, and dwell in the uttermost
>   parts of the sea
> Even there shall thy hand lead me,
>   and thy right hand shall hold me (verses 7–9).

Salvation consists in 'getting right with God' or co-operating with the inner process of individuation. That is the individual and personal task of every man. It is inseparable from the ethical task which is that of assisting others towards the same salvation. Therefore the only absolute moral and spiritual law is to do nothing which either impedes one's own process of sanctification or interferes with the progress of anyone else. This is only a new expression of the old commandment about loving God and loving my neighbour as myself. It includes the commandment that I should not cause my neighbour to stumble (Rom. 14.21).

In the service to our neighbour, which is the stuff of Christian morality, we help by presenting ourselves to him in forms which correspond outwardly to the archetypal aspects which constitute his inwardness. So we have seen the rôles of Shadow and anima/animus in this task. But our highest duty and our most important task is to provide our neighbour with living images of his own Self. In the traditional religious language this means that we are to behave in such a way that the love of God is revealed in us (I John 4.11–12,20). How can we do this since we are not perfect?

The answer is that we can do so only by grace. If we remain open to the love and grace of God, that is if we allow ourselves to be developed and shaped by the integrating forces of the unconscious while at the same time consciously co-operating with their movements, then what is constantly being wrought in us will slowly but surely become visible to our neighbour. The saints are

those who have done this supremely. Our vocation is to be like
them. Few will actually achieve the success of the saints but the
vocation is the same for all of us. The call is to sanctity, to
wholeness, to that perfect balance in our souls which alone is able
to reveal the vision of God. The parent represents the Self as father
to the child and the old man full of years and wisdom personifies
the same Self to the inexperienced young man. That is why what
kind of parents we are is important; as it is also important, not just
for ourselves but for those under our influence, how we grow old
and how we face death. Each one of us personifies the Self for those
of the next generation and the generation after that. So we must
take care what kind of Self we become, for the old man broken,
wretched and afraid or the old woman whining, cantankerous and
neurotic present only images of chaos and dissociation to those
who come after. That is the moral significance of the doctrine of
hell.

Whereas Christ's commandment is 'Be ye therefore perfect,
even as your Father which is in heaven is perfect' (Matt. 5.48).
But we can only become perfect images of the Self by our acceptance
of the work of that same Self among the basic structures of our
personality. And that is simply another way of expressing the old
truth that we are saved only by the grace of God.

Conclusion: Being Saved

Being saved, then, is not something which happens once and for all when we go forward at a revival meeting or when we feel our heart 'strangely warmed' in a quiet chapel or by our own bedside. Neither is it something that can be airily dismissed as 'emotional nonsense' by the intellectual liberal in all his exquisite sophistication. Being saved is what happens to us when we see in our inner life and in our social life a pattern of spiritual development which is the life of Christ.

Like him, we shall experience initiation, temptation, occasional encouragements but also loneliness and final dereliction. But not quite final, for we shall also experience resurrection. We experience all these things already as the separate aspects and forces of our personality are brought together in some sort of harmony and balance and as we learn to live with others.

None of this is a simple matter of striving to be good or of pretending to 'faith'. It is a subtle inward movement of which we are usually quite unconscious and its nature is better described by words such as 'passivity' and 'acceptance' than words like 'striving' and 'decision'. We shall need to make decisions and we shall be called upon to do a certain amount of striving but our salvation does not depend upon these things: that is the meaning of 'grace'.

The most difficult truth of which we need to persuade ourselves is that God does really love us, and he is constantly trying to reveal his love in us. Or, in psychological terms, integration and wholeness is always possible because our being, though it contains many aspects, is a unity. To be aware of the spiritual journey is itself part of being saved. Even, especially, the pain and poignancy of the journey. Agony and ecstasy are not infinitely apart but infinitely close. Crucifixion and resurrection are never separated.

We must learn to accept and to affirm. Yes to all that has been. Yes to all that is to come. That is abundant life: the life of Christ, the life of the soul. We cannot see all that lies in store for us, our final destiny. How can the soul of man possess what is infinite – except in the microcosm of our own personality we play out the eternal drama of creation. The miracle is that this happens in each and every life. So there is here in the body of this flesh a true intimation of final perfection – an intimation which is itself part of the final perfection. Or as Paul said, 'Now we see through a glass darkly; but then face to face: now I know in part; but then I shall know even as I am known.'